CASE STUDIES IN AUTISM

CASE STUDIES IN
AUTISM

A Young Child and Two Adolescents

Cheryl D. Seifert

Edited by Charlene Breedlove

UNIVERSITY
PRESS OF
AMERICA

Lanham • New York • London

University Press of America®, Inc.

4720 Boston Way
Lanham, Maryland 20706

3 Henrietta Street
London WC2E 8LU England

Library of Congress Cataloging-in-Publication Data

Seifert, Cheryl D.
Case studies in autism : a young child and
two adolescents / Cheryl D. Seifert.
p.   cm.
Includes bibliographical references (p.)
1. Autism—Case studies.   I. Title.
RJ506.A9S43   1990   616.89'8209—dc20   89–25098 CIP

ISBN 0–8191–7722–9 (alk. paper)
ISBN 0–8191–7723–7 (pbk. : alk. paper)

 The paper used in this publication meets the minimum requirements of
American National Standard for Information Sciences—Permanence
of Paper for Printed Library Materials, ANSI Z39.48–1984.

To Theodore C. Seifert, Jr.
and
Eleanore S. Seifert

Contents

1

Infantile Autism

Autism can be one of the most serious psychopathologies a child and his or her family endures. Usually, autistic children are born, to all appearances, physiologically and psychologically sound, with normal facies and an intelligent expression. Their gross motor development tends to proceed normally: the child begins walking at the appropriate time and, around 18 months of age, parents look forward to hearing the first sounds of articulate speech. Not until the child fails to speak do parents become anxious and risk asking the terrible question: why? The experience of learning their child is autistic can be heartbreaking; up till now, they have had no reason to believe their child's development would be other than perfectly normal.

Unless parents are alerted by the subtle early signs of autism in the infant's development, for instance, by infrequent or excessive crying, not reaching out to be held or the body suddenly stiffening when held, an indifference to sensory stimulation and companionship—all cues that an untrained observer might easily overlook—parents are not likely to realize that something is amiss. Not until the age of 18 months do the symptoms of autism become starkly evident. One begins to see a willfully averted gaze and specific kinds of repetitious, stereotypical behavior such as walking on tiptoes, flapping arms when excited, finger flicking, and playing with toys in an obsessively fixed routine.

Probably in an attempt to control the environment by making it more predictable and thus easier to cope with, the autistic child prefers to play in rigidly structured patterns that leave no room for flexibility and imagination. He (for 3 to 1 autistic children are male) may sit for hours day after day aligning the same objects in identical arrangements, becoming distressed if the order is in the least changed. Play materials of choice include neatly structured items such as routes, timetables, numbers, or geometric designs of similar form and visual pattern, which become objects of great attention and attachment. People are of as little interest to the autistic child as are his surroundings and he prefers to be alone as much as possible.

The autistic child's social withdrawal, unusual choice of play objects, and lack of communication leave parents uncertain how to respond. Rearing an autistic child is extremely difficult and a negative feedback circuit can develop between parent and child, wherein the child receives inappropriate reactions from the mother if she perceives the child's behavior as inadequate. Or, to protect the child, the mother may permit him to withdraw, and unknowingly promote the disorder.

Autism has been recognized as a disorder for about 45 years, having been first identified by Leo Kanner (1943) as "disturbances of affective contact." In other words, fundamental to autism is a severe disjunction in the child's ability to relate to other people. In the years since Kanner's seminal paper, much progress has been made toward understanding the etiology of autism, a disorder that occurs in all parts of the world, in all races, and in all types of families. Compared prevalence studies in England, Wales, the United States, and Denmark show that about three fourths of autistic children are male, with a total population prevalence rate of approximately five children per 10,000 (Brask 1970; Lotter 1966; Treffert 1970).

There was a time, from 1943 to 1971, when researchers believed the disorder occurred more frequently in higher socioeconomic groups and portrayed the parents of autistic children as unstimulating, aloof, and lacking in real warmth. We now realize, however, that such notions are scientifically unsupported. To the parents of autistic children born during that time was added the burden of guilt. To this day, no social or psychological characteristics of parents or families have been proved to be associated with autism in such a way that they could conceivably induce the disorder. (For a historical review of the subject see *Theories of Autism* [Seifert 1990a].)

Although precise connections between various organic conditions and the symptoms of autism remain unclear, the evidence accumulated so far points to an underlying organic cause. For example, autism has been observed in association with a variety of organic abnormalities— neurological, genetic, and metabolic illnesses, and structural brain abnormalities such as phenylketonuria, congenital rubella, celiac disease, tuberous sclerosis, purine disorder, toxoplasmosis, congenital syphilis, encephalitis, infantile spasms, Cornelia deLange syndrome, and cytomegalic inclusion disease, and still others. In a few patients, abnormalities that occur early in brain development have been detected in portions of the cerebellum, a part of the brain involved in helping regulate motion and some aspects of memory (Courchesne et al. 1988), and in the limbic system, a part of the brain involved in the emotions, together with a deficiency of Purkinje cells in those brain regions (Bauman and Kemper 1985). About 20% of autistic children develop seizures by age 18; the peak period of onset is between 11 and 14 years. Many also show unusual reflexes, abnormal EEGs, and abnormal left-hemisphere function, which suggest the presence of an underlying neurological disorder, perhaps in the structure of cortical neurons, thalamocortical connections, or brainstem. In computerized x-rays (CT scans) of the brains of some autistic children the width of the third ventricle increases with age (Hoshino et al. 1984). An enlargement of the ventricles' fluid-filled cavities within the brain can indicate atrophy of other brain structures. These findings may suggest a progressive disorder of the thalamus, hypothalamus, or mid-brain surrounding the third ventricle, possibly leading to epileptic seizures or the loss of intellectual and motor abilities as the child ages.

In the last five years, studies have shown positive evidence of hereditary influences (Brown et al. 1982; Blomquist et al. 1985). Some cases of autism appear to be associated with the fragile-X syndrome, an anomaly of one sex chromosome. Generally, however, it is probably not autism as such that is inherited, but broader language and cognitive abnormalities of which autism is one particular manifestation. All in all, there is a consensus that autism represents some form of organic brain dysfunction but that no single factor underlies all cases; rather, various extents and types of brain abnormalities and injury may lead to the same autistic disorder. (For a theoretical framework in which to study autism, see *Holistic Interpretation of Autism: A Theoretical Framework* [Seifert 1990b].)

IDENTIFYING AUTISM

One of the major problems confronting the psychological field has been establishing strict guidelines by which to diagnose the autistic syndrome. Historically, the terminology designating disorders generally grouped as ''early childhood psychosis,'' namely infantile autism, childhood schizophrenia, early infantile psychosis, and symbiotic psychosis, has been used with gross inconsistency. As a consequence, the literature has not been statistically clean and misdiagnoses have led to errors in sample selection and misinterpretation of important research as late as 1978. Individual investigators have had their own ideas regarding etiology, ranging from the psychological (poor parenting) to the neurological (either genetic or due to birth defect) to interactive explanations. Adding to the confusion, many frequently used terms meant different things to different people. Thus a variety of categorical systems accumulated and a muddle of overlapping diagnoses thrived. Therapy was just as idiosyncratic: treatments ranged from separating the child from its parents, psychoanalysis, to electric shock therapy. Meanwhile, parents floundered in their search for a way to help their child.

Today the pivotal question is, do autistic children differ in any way from children with schizophrenia or those mentally retarded? Studies have shown that they do. In the mentally retarded there are often behavioral abnormalities similar to those seen in autism, but the full syndrome of infantile autism is rarely present. (It is within the mentally retarded group of below 50 IQ that diagnosis is most likely to vary; severely retarded children show more autisticlike features, but not the full syndrome.) In schizophrenic children there are also oddities of behavior, but typically these are hallucinations, delusions, and loosening of associations or incoherence, none of which is present in autism. Autistic children also differ from those with schizophrenia in that the latter tend to cling to adults, whereas autistic children are generally physically unresponsive; schizophrenic children are usually poorly coordinated, whereas autistic children engage in movements requiring a high degree of dexterity; schizophrenic children are more likely than autistic children to come from families with a history of schizophrenia, and the onset of symptoms is usually much later for schizophrenia than for autism. The prognosis is usually better for schizophrenic children than it is for the autistic. Some parents report their children having been given dual diagnoses of autism and aphasia, a language disorder. In developmental language disorders, however, children generally make eye contact and will often try to communicate by means of gestures. We are now beginning to see the distinctions between autism and other psychiatric and developmental disorders much more clearly.

BEHAVIORAL CHARACTERISTICS

As we enter the 1990s, the situation surrounding efforts to define autism has dramatically improved. The Professional Advisory Board of the Autism Society of America formulated a definition of the autistic syndrome that represents a consensus among professionals from different countries and disciplines, which formed the basis for a similar definition published in the revised third edition of the American Psychiatric Association's *Diagnostic and Statistical Manual of Mental Disorders* (1987). The new definition contradicts traditional thoughts about autism and requires revising our current understanding. The new definition led to the now generally accepted position that infantile autism is a developmental disorder accompanied by severe and, to a large extent, permanent intellectual and social deficits.

Despite therapeutic intervention, the autistic child fails to develop reciprocal social interactions, communication skills, and imaginative activity. Such children appear to be affectless, their faces at an early age frequently register a blank stare or an out-of-touch expression on one side of the face and a more in-touch expression on the other side. Yet, these children do not lack feelings, rather their emotive expression is masked by their withdrawal. Persistently the child will ignore people. Due probably to organic brain dysfunction, the child responds hypersensitively to every kind of auditory, visual, and tactile stimulation and makes great effort, often by covering his ears and burying his head in his arms, to reduce this painful excess, especially when it is generated by social contact. He tries to shut out his environment, which in turn leads to further withdrawal and failure to relate to people in all but the most minimal ways. To mobilize their reactions, to become aroused, usually requires an intense situation. Slapstick comedy and rough-house play sometimes will do it. Even when older, the autistic child remains aloof and literal-minded, without social judgment and empathy toward others' feelings and responses. The chief question in discussions of affect and cognition in the autistic child is whether cognitive problems are central to autism. Or, as one research group believes (Fein et al. 1986), are social deficits primary and actually the key symptom of the disorder?

About 50% of autistic children never speak. Those who do may utter a few sounds but the sounds often do not evolve into words. If speech does develop, so do characteristic abnormalities. For example, autistic children are not able to select appropriate personal pronouns, frequently speaking of themselves as "you" and the person addressed as "I," confusing the object and subject of discourse. They also speak echolalically, repeating verbatim a sentence or series of sentences they have heard. These impoverished utterances at times seem to be triggered by some similarity conjured by the situation in which the speech was first heard. Speech comprehension and expression may be limited to concretions, usually nouns. The most verbal autistic children use correct verb tense only about 8% of the time.

The severe language impairment in autistic children seems to be related to a generally impaired ability to think symbolically and representationally and sustain an abstract attitude. The autistic child is bound to the concrete sensorimotor stage of development; out of sight objects and people cease to exist. A mother does not exist when she leaves the room; a toy does not exist when it is blocked from view. This continues past 8 months of age, when such behavior ceases in the normal child, and into childhood.

Autistic children also lack symbolic gestures and the ability to pantomime. When asked to point or show by nonverbal gestures, they are unable. Instead, they will make their need known by taking someone by the wrist (not usually by the grasped hand). Most striking of all is their failure to use what speech they do have or a nonverbal gesture for social communication. In older autistic children, abnormality in speech rhythms, neologisms, omissions, and idiosyncratic, context inappropriate word usages are common.

IQ tests of autistic children have demonstrated a wide variety of intellectual functions, from the severely retarded (approximately 75% of all autistic people function in the retarded range throughout life) to normal. In general, autistic people test higher in perceptual–motor and motor tasks than in verbal tasks. Lowest scores are in abstract verbal reasoning and highest scores in fitting and assembly tasks. About one tenth have remarkable idiot savant abilities. One autistic boy whom this author studied into adolescence could multiply two three-digit numbers in his head and cite the specific day of the week a particular calendar date fell in a given year. Other autistic children show extraordinary musical, artistic, and memory abilities. To recapitulate, there are wide individual differences between autistic children and apparent inconsistencies within each child.

TREATMENT

Drug treatment of autistic children has proved difficult on two counts: its uncertain efficacy and the numerous side effects that result from prolonged exposure in children who cannot communicate physical discomfort such as dry mouth, dizziness, or allergic reactions. Stimulants, psychedelics, antidepressants, antipsychotic agents, and other drugs have been used and studied in autistic children. While some of these agents have been associated with behavioral improvements in some individuals, for instance, decreased hyperactivity, decreased withdrawal and stereotyped behaviors, and decreased sleep disturbances, no group of drugs is clearly superior in treating autism; improvement may occur in some areas at the same time others are aggravated.

During the last 20 years, the most significant development in the treatment of autism has been in the use of behavioral education. Special education in a structured environment appears to promote language and social development. Treatment in a one-to-one teacher-child relationship has proved most beneficial, but too costly for most institutions and school programs.

Behavior modification (reinforcements and punishments) appears to increase social behavior and decrease maladaptive behavior. Some researchers advocate electric skin shock (Lovaas, Schreibman, and Koegel 1974) to suppress self-abusive activity; others call for more drastic measures, such as applying an automatic vapor ammonia spray (Rojahn et al. 1987), or static noise emitted through earphones, known as aversion therapy. Although many therapists hesitate to use such techniques and decry these methods as unnecessary, unconstructive, and inhumane, others, frustrated by years of unsuccessful treatments, have turned to controversial programs of behavior modification.

Occasional reports of an autistic adult marrying, having children, and living a successful life will always be found to reflect either an incorrect diagnosis or a variation of the disorder. While most therapeutic advances will lead to progress in the child's general social and behavioral development, they are not a cure for autism. In terms of achieving a self-supportive adulthood, the typical prognostic picture is poor. About two thirds of autistic individuals are unable to care for themselves; about 5% to 17% achieve a borderline independent status, are working and leading some kind of social life. At best, if the initial IQ is over 60 or 70 and if there are expressive language skills by age 5, the child has about a 50/50 chance of achieving a fair social adjustment in adult life. Even the autistic child with the most favorable prognosis has only a 1% or 2% chance of becoming completely normal.[1]

METHOD

The traditional way for therapists to communicate their studies of autistic children, and those with other interesting and important symptoms associated with organic disorder, has been to describe, in careful detail, a single case observed over a long period of time—a practice all too rare today. The following observations, derived from a four-year study of an autistic child, show how, through observation and the expressive channels of art, we can better recognize and understand the symptoms and signs of psychopathology. The case study method also may shed light on the question of how the brain affected by organic lesion compensates for the effects of brain disorder.

I chose this case study for several reasons. First, the case of Brian meets American Psychiatric Association diagnostic criteria for autism; the diagnosis was confirmed by the Department of Child Psychiatry of the University of Chicago and one other major medical center. Second, I found in Brian's behavioral responses during these years a convincing illustration of the central cognitive and affective disorders involved in autism. Third, the case of Brian has the unique value of demonstrating what can happen to an autistic child under some of the best possible conditions: Brian had a concerned and stable family and he received therapeutic intervention very early in life.

2

Case Study of a Young Child

While working in the section for dysfunctioning children at Michael Reese Hospital, Chicago, for a medical geneticist from the University of Chicago, I had a splendid opportunity to "get my feet wet" in his clinics. To a psychologist trained in a research setting with a clinical component, the appeal of observing research patients was high, and for eight weeks my time was undividedly given to a small hospital day-school program whose goal was to evaluate, diagnose, and educate rare nonverbal behavioral disordered children excluded from public school settings.

Being unstressed by clinical routines, I focused daily attention on a young autistic child with whom I casually spent time, interacting, presenting formal and informal material and tests, and just watching and wondering about. I considered Brian, aged 3 years, "raw material." He had been recently diagnosed autistic, and was on the brink of beginning formal education, albeit in a hospital-based program. My assignment was to evaluate him and provide a viable treatment plan.

The following is a summary description of what actually took place in my psychotherapeutic treatment of Brian.

HISTORY

General eye-to-eye contact was almost completely absent initially, except for a fleeting gaze on my first approach to Brian. I attempted bonding procedures by joining in something that interested him at the moment (and by communicating this nonverbally). Knowing that typical bonding techniques and social games, such as pat-a-cake, peek-a-

9

boo, and ball rolling, failed to engage the autistic child, I did not attempt these until termination of contact with Brian became inevitable. They failed here, as they have elsewhere.

By accident, Brian and I developed a social game around perfume. He was fascinated by the scent of a perfume bottle I brought out from a drawer. Having obviously had little previous experience with such a scent, he became momentarily engrossed in social play around smelling perfume and for the first time responded to me. I held the perfume bottle for him to smell and took turns smelling, enforcing no eye contact and no speech. Predictably and silently, at each therapy session the perfume appeared from a drawer and disappeared back into it. No speech, no eye contact, and no overt gesturing were attempted on my part for many sessions. I found that wearing the same color scheme, usually white, including a laboratory coat, seemed to accelerate familiarity and ease identification and acceptance. Gradual, delicate intrusions and tracking his interests seemed effective in preventing Brian's total withdrawal and increasing social interaction. A concrete approach that was nonaggressive, nonthreatening, and extremely patient resulted in Brian's interest in communication and a pleasant, fruitful enterprise between us.

In accordance with my assessment of the biosocial nature of autism, the therapy I used was based on ethological concepts suggested by Niko Tinbergen (Tinbergen and Tinbergen 1972). Tinbergen emphasizes a continuum between normal and autistic children, viewing autistic symptomatology as a variant of normal behavior. His approach combines the finely detailed observations of the ethological method and studies of approach–withdrawal courtship behavior in gulls with an encounter with an autistic child.

The observations that autistic children have decreased tendencies to approach others and increased tendencies to withdraw in social situations, but have some capacity for interpersonal behavior, were implemented in my treatment approach to Brian (Kramer, Anderson, and Westman 1984). I did this by observing and mirroring his approach patterns; when, for instance, he initiated eye contact, turned his head toward me, smiled, altered the space between us, initiated physical contact or verbal interaction, I responded accordingly. Following Tinbergen's (1972) ethological model of autism, I graded Brian's approach behavior from socially positive, such as making eye contact with me, to socially negative, such as burying his head in his arms or averting his gaze.

My early experience in individual therapy sessions with Brian taught me that he interacted primarily using socially negative behavior; through a nonintrusive, mirroring approach, he spent more and more time in socially positive ways. Nonintrusive interactions were used primarily to avoid stimulating withdrawal behavior in which fear might become the mediating emotion (Tinbergen and Tinbergen 1972). Thus, to Brian's long periods of withdrawn behavior, I responded by mirroring such behavior. I considered his bizarre behavior to mean stay away. He became neither more withdrawn nor more stereotypic in his behavior. Finally, he returned to a more interactive process that included eye contact.

During a four-year period, by separating individual steps into their communicative and affective components, Brian's therapy evolved into helping develop his affective experiences and his comprehension of interpersonal situations and social signals. Through mirroring bodily contact and intensive displays of simple emotions, Brian and I worked into his playing together with others for the first time. However, Brian never progressed beyond making primitive social contact; the far-reaching retardation in his language and social development was evident in his failure to use language.

From ages 3 to 7, Brian produced a multitude of drawings, a mode of communication that required no verbal skill, yet provided some basis for judging social perception and cognitive abilities. Because of the huge quantity of Brian's drawings, I chose to concentrate on his human-figure drawings.

While I was with him, Brian continually engaged in an active and intense effort to withdraw. Since one of his problems was a deeply disrupted body image, it was not surprising that the subject least likely to be drawn was the human figure.

Identifying the Syndrome

Brian had been brought to me by his mother and father for psychological evaluation. They complained that Brian spoke only a few words. His speech and language development was alarmingly subnormal, and he had little interest in people. He was unable to follow the regular school curriculum or learn by instruction like a normal child. The parents were concerned about his behavioral peculiarities and the fact that he had never shown interest in his surroundings or in normal childhood activity.

Brian had yet to develop any communicative speech; what speech he had was mostly imitative echoes of television commercials. He was precocious at figuring out how to do certain things for himself (e.g., getting into cupboards), but when he could not do something he wanted, he would try to enlist one of his parents to do it for him. Otherwise, Brian avoided most contact or interaction. His favorite pastime was watching television commercials, being drawn to the television set from anywhere in the house by the sound of a commercial jingle. He particularly enjoyed facial close-ups, at which he babbled excitedly. His activity level was variable and high. He seemed constantly to be moving his hands, his legs, and other parts of his body. His behavior was random and purposeless. Neurological examination showed Brian to have a normal electroencephalogram record and no signs of neurological disturbance.

Original observations made by this author between Brian's ages 3 and 7 (the years 1978 to 1982) will appear in italics. Photographs of Brian's infancy were provided by his parents.

Brian is a tiny, well-proportioned boy who displays essentially a flawless appearance with no physical anomalies and an intelligent face. He shows strong gaze aversion, burying his head during social encounters. His attitude toward people is rejecting, with an expressionless look aimed past another's eyes. He has a sense of well-being, as motorically and otherwise self-absorbed and socially aloof.

Brian wanders in circles in the center of the room, flapping his hands and fixing on nothing in particular. He walks on tiptoe and tends to posture. He has no words, but a multitude of spontaneous sounds. He flinches when approached, and shows little affect.

Brian takes no notice of the three adults present in the small room where the consultation takes place. The father tries to interest him in some of the toys, but Brian steers around him without looking at him or even seeming to notice him ("like I'm one of the chairs," says the father). Brian permits his mother to pick him up but does not acknowledge her either. Then he gets down off her lap and resumes his circling. Eventually he picks up his mother's purse and begins playing with it, taking things out one by one, then putting them back, over and over again. The mother takes the purse away, and Brian gives a high-pitched whimper and begins flapping his hands. After a few minutes, he sits down and begins arranging his dominoes in rows. Several times the doctor tries to place the next domino for him but he flaps his hands or places them over his ears and then removes the domino that was placed. When the parents begin to leave and the mother moves toward the door, Brian (again without seeming to notice her) takes up a position directly in front of the door so that it cannot be opened. The mother places him back in the center of the room and leaves. After a minute of whimpering with his hands over his ears, Brian sits down to the dominoes again. When his father leaves, the scene is repeated. Then Brian breaks out crying and tries to open the door. When he cannot, he takes the doctor's hand and tries to use it (like a tool) to open the door. The doctor picks him up to console him; he permits this without response.

Once again in his parents' presence, Brian calms down but gives no other sign that they are there. Subsequently, he again occupies himself in repetitive play and is upset when someone attempts to intrude or participate. Then, as previously described, he undoes the intrusion, if possible, but takes no other notice of the adult. He does, however, seem progressively less upset when left alone and is soothed by being picked up, bounced, and spoken to.

Brian, an only child, was born at Presbyterian-St. Luke's Hospital, Chicago, 28 September 1975. He was the product of a full-term pregnancy, throughout which the mother experienced rather severe nausea and occasional vomiting. He was delivered by cesarean section under general anesthesia (dystocia) after a prolonged labor of 26 hours (hard labor about 24 hours). His birth weight was 7 pounds, 3 ounces. He cried immediately, and there were no problems in the nursery. With the exception of colds, his health record has been good.

Brian's mother became extremely concerned about overt manifestations of unusual personality when he was about 2 years of age. She made careful observations of his behavior at successive stages of his development, and presented him to several psychologists, psychiatrists, and neurologists at the University of Chicago, Departments of Pediatrics and Psychiatry, during his third year and every two years for follow-up, offering her own data and information from Brian's teachers.

The family background presents a history of two distant paternal cousins who were born with congenital anomalies—one with hydrocephalus, the other with questionable rubella syndrome—and a paternal aunt with lupus. Brian's paternal grandfather is deceased; the paternal grandmother lives nearby. Brian's father is a mechanical engineer and an intellectually quick, warm, friendly man, dedicated to his

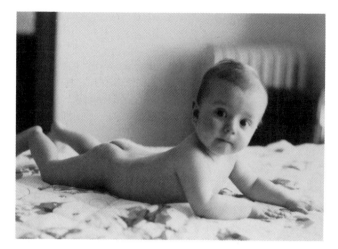

Figure 2-1. Brian, age 8 months.

family. He is Czechoslovakian-American. Brian's maternal grandfather was an erudite physician, founder and director of the School of Medicine, University of Bolivia; the maternal grandmother was a former opera singer from Chile. Both maternal grandparents were ambidextrous. Brian's mother is a former accountant who is pleasant and caring. She was born in Bolivia, lived 11½ years in New York City, and speaks Spanish and English fluently. Her intelligence is above average and she has devoted most of the last three years to Brian's education.

First and Second Years

The only abnormality noticed during Brian's first year was difficulty in feeding (Fig. 2-1). He was nursed originally, but switched to a bottle at 3 months old. Toward the end of the first year, weaning from the bottle was unsuccessfully attempted. At 2½ years old, he bit through the nipple but would not accept a new one. (By this time he was taking some solid foods.) He began to drink from a cup, but shuddered at the sight of white milk. The problem was solved by adding Ovaltine. He "nibbled through his food," taking a long time to eat.

He slept regularly through the night without waking. He was on a demand-feeding schedule and his mother attended to his slightest fret immediately. She carried him a lot and changed his diapers frequently. He was always limp and passive when picked up, avoided eye contact,

Figure 2-2. Left, Brian, age 10½ months, shows beginnings of symptomatic motor behavior and low body tone. *Right,* age 13 months, with open hand grasp.

and was sometimes upset by physical contact. He was a quiet, sweet child, and smiled often.

At about 6 months old, he made speech sounds and his parents considered him mentally alert. His first tooth came at 6 months old. He sat alone at 7 months, stood up at 10 months, and walked at 12 months of age. The beginnings of symptomatic motor behavior (Fig. 2-2) were observed at 10½ months as Brian exhibited a low body tone in a sitting position.

Retardation was first suspected at 18 months, for he talked no more than he did at 6 months. He was well-developed and well-nourished, but small, being in the tenth percentile for weight. His head circumference was 49 cm (in the fiftieth percentile). He is ambidextrous and had uncertain eye dominance. He followed some simple commands.

Third Year

It became evident that Brian never really looked happy; his smile was not fully given. He did not appear to listen, although his hearing was normal. He showed discomfort with conversation on television and used his mother's hand to change the television channel. He failed to form any discernible words, saying "mamamamama" over and over again. He was toilet trained in one month's time and has had no relapses. As to diet, he preferred fruits and did not like sweets. He would not take a cookie or candy. He got his own food and climbed heights to do so. He continued to be undemanding. He seldom cried

Figure 2-3. Brian, age 21 months, plays inappropriately with his bicycle. He immediately turns it over to rotate the wheels repetitiously.

but screamed when he did not get his way. He seemed easily frightened by others. He repeated the same task over and over, and spent long periods of time on one activity, completing puzzles quickly and spinning the wheels of a toy car ("he could do this for hours," his mother says; Figs. 2-3 and 2-4). He abounded in symptomatic motor behavior (Fig. 2-5). He walked on his toes and flapped his hands when excited. He began his schooling at Michael Reese Hospital in Chicago in a special day-school program for nonverbal children and received daily play therapy, arousal- and attention-oriented schooling to increase his ability to stay in contact with the environment.

Fourth and Fifth Years

Brian showed the first sign of a remarkable interest in shapes, letters, numbers, paper-pencil tasks and reading. He liked musical rhythm and sang along with recordings. He used the typewriter and took hold of the tape recorder and camera and tried to make them function. Social development is subnormal, and he did not dress himself, nor did he interact with other people. He preferred to eat with his hands but used a spoon and fork when coaxed. He swam and dove into deep water and rode a tricycle. He attempted to throw a ball, but with no strength. His running was uncoordinated (a dainty hop), and he used his arms like flippers.

Figure 2-4. Brian, age 2 years, 4 months, lines up objects, stares.

Figure 2-5. Left, symptomatic motor behavior at 3 years of age. Walking on
tiptoe in on-guard position, hands held open in a fixed position to
maintain stability. *Upper right,* a typical position: legs stretched
out, hands flapping, left leg lifted. *Lower right,* motor behavior
appears "stiff."

Figure 2-6. Left, Brian, age 4 years, draws a picture of a human figure while engaged in an intense effort to withdraw socially. Through his drawing he reveals how he looked at people. *Figure 2-7. Right,* a drawing by a normal child, age 4 years.

I had no way of determining what was going on in Brian's mind, until, at age 4, without any previous scribbling, his first drawing erupted in the classroom. Schematic though it was, it was the first indication that he was aware of his surroundings and attempting communication. With quick fluency and minimal line, the drawing showed a discernible face (Fig. 2-6).

Brian had drawn a mental image of a face as an 8-month-old infant might have perceived one. Whereas most children's drawings (Fig. 2-7) at age 4 already represent conceptual attributes of the person, though without visual perspective (Luquet 1927), Brian functioned at a sensorimotor level (Piaget [1936] 1952) and was unable to represent an absent object.

Brian was indifferent to human beings, being absorbed only in inanimate objects and stereotyped behaviors. At age 5, he developed an obsessive preoccupation with letters and numbers, displaying phenomenal memory, spelling, and reading ability, but without comprehension or communicative speech (Fig. 2-8). His inclination to invest in objects can be seen in the aridity with which he memorized addresses and lottery numbers, and drew calendars. He knew songs and books by heart before he could read, though Brian never seemed to be aware of or take pride in the extraordinary character of his feats as might a normal child.

Figure 2-8. Brian, age 6 years, brings about affect in a self-stimulating activity and draws "thrilling" numbers. He shows a sense of composition; his numbers center around a pinnacle.

A number of questions arise. How are we to assess and explain the discrepancies in achievements and personality structure found in autistic children and in those with idiot savant abilities (Scheerer, Rothmann, and Goldstein 1945), with central aphasia (Myklebust 1954), with mixed transcortical aphasia (Geschwind, Quadfasel, and Segarra 1968), and hyperlexia (Huttenlocher and Huttenlocher 1973)? How can it be that a profound retardate appears normal, indeed supernormal, in some specificities and yet subnormal in practically all others? And how does this fact harmonize with the lack of normal capacity to learn, even in those fields where skill is demonstrated?

These questions are rooted in personality development, which remains puzzling for theorists because of the many interrelated biological and environmental factors involved. A qualitative analysis of Brian's intelligence, language, and affect are needed to better understand the nature of his defective functioning.

MEASURES OF INTELLIGENCE

Psychological tests administered at 4 years of age yield an IQ of 51 on the Cattell (1940) and Stanford-Binet (Terman and Merrill 1973; S-B Form L-M) intelligence scales, and 116 on the Leiter International

Performance Scale (Leiter 1969a, 1969b). Brian's performance in some of the subtests seems hampered by his inability to understand or use language.

Brian's IQ of 51 remains stationary from his 4th to 7th year, placing him at the mildly retarded level. His cognitive functioning is highly atypical of children in general, and he shows a great discrepancy between verbal and nonverbal abilities. Profoundly retarded in language development, and borderline retarded in motor development, Brian shows normal ability on one measure: perceptual discrimination skill. Although the Binet scoring does not focus on qualitative intellectual functions, an intelligence profile characteristic of autistic children can be derived from Brian's successes and failures on the subtests.

On the Cattell Infant Intelligence Scale (Cattell 1940), at age 4, Brian's basal age is 12 months. He passes only certain tests on the S-B II and S-B III-year level, none above the S-B III, except *forms* at S-B IV, *patience rectangles* at S-B V (Terman and Merrill 1973), and *visual-discrimination* for color, shape, and position at Leiter IX (Leiter 1969a, 1969b). He succeeds on all levels in tasks involving:

1. simple form and spatial relations (form board; patience rectangles; visual matching);
2. visual motor and immediate memory (reproducing a bead chain; circle, S-B III).

He fails when the tasks require:

1. imitation (imitating placing a cube in or over a cup; imitating beating a spoon; imitating hitting a doll);
2. object permanence (uncovering a toy);
3. verbal association (naming an object and defining it in terms of use, categorization);
4. comprehension (commands);
5. complex form and spatial relations (comparing sticks, building a block bridge, copying a square).

Brian is highly visually perceptive, and he succeeds within a context of limited choices involving shape and color. His perceptual matching skill develops without abstract association (Figs. 2-9, 2-10, and 2-11).

Two years later, at 6 years and 1 month, testing essentially shows the same intelligence profile and accentuates the above findings. Brian fails as before on tasks involving logical relations in the verbal or spatial sphere. He is successful in tests requiring associative memory, immediate retention, and simple visual discrimination. He shows de-

V - 1

Genus

Figure 2-9. Typical failure response. Conceptual task allows grouping according to common class or genus, i.e., flower, animal, fruit, etc., depending on the representation process. (Used by permission, Leiter 1969a.)

VIII - 2

Form Discrimination

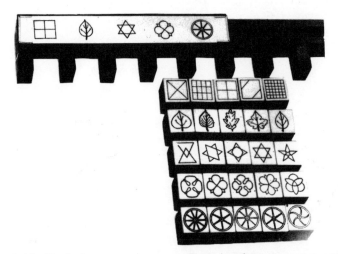

Figure 2-10. Typical success response. Task involves sameness and symmetry and evaluates perceptual discrimination. Some conceptualization of color class, size, and position might be present, but it is restricted to a context of limited choices, e.g., matching. (Used by permission, Leiter 1969a.)

Figure 2-11. Brian, age 4 years, 1 month, begins his task. He readies himself, blissfully, by making blowing sounds, "wheww . . .
wheww . . . ," raising his arms, and twiddling his fingers.

pressed verbal ability and areas of good nonverbal ability, without the
typical motor deficits present with anoxia and common childhood illnesses affecting the brain.

Atypical features of Brian's cognitive abilities are not reflected in
the quantification of his IQ. However, systematizing observations of
his behavior, using Piaget's stages of infant cognition, pinpoints
Brian's deficits and their interrelatedness.

Sensorimotor Intelligence

From 3 to 7 years of age, Brian is in a sensorimotor stage of
intelligence. He is in a state of disequilibrium or disadaptation, and is
not accommodating to reality; assimilation is out of control. As he fails
to accommodate to the real world, his autistic symptoms become more
apparent.

Since Brian is in the sensorimotor stage of cognitive development,
he functions like an infant during its first 24 months of life. He only
understands sensorimotor activity and makes sense out of his environment through looking, listening, manipulating, and moving his body.
He focuses only on the immediate situation, unable to make mental
representations of absent objects and events distant in time. He is just

beginning to understand perceptually an object, cause and effect, space, and time. In most aspects, his cognitive functioning is less than that of an 8- or 9-month-old infant.

Having not developed the object concept, expected at the 9-month level (Cattell 1940), Brian does not realize that objects are permanent and are moved by forces that have nothing to do with his behavior toward them. This is typified by the way he shows interest in a toy car—his favorite object. When the car is removed from the table where he sits, he turns unperturbed to some other interesting sight, not realizing that the toy continues to exist although he cannot see it.

The comings and goings of people also pass unnoticed. Like a 5-month-old infant, he thinks that if one mother leaves, another one will pop up somewhere. Only when he discovers that he has only one mother and his perceptual system sufficiently matures, in turn affecting his cognitive development, does a pattern of interaction between his mother and himself begin. And then he begins to protest when his mother goes away.

Brian, at age 4, has not developed the separation of means and ends (causes and effects) expected at the 14-month level (Cattell 1940). He shows few deliberate efforts to bring about desired changes in his environment or to cause things to happen. He does not forcefully try to remove any barrier between him and an object such as a favorite toy, and he loses interest if such an obstacle is interposed. He readily turns away from a favorite pastime if there is any interference. He shows no persistent effort to focus on a goal, and no sign of behavioral intention. He demonstrates no separation of means and ends, such as pushing a book away to reach his car.

He repeats a single attempt to prolong an act that produces a fortuitous effect, such as opening and closing the refrigerator door 300 times a day—showing the beginning of circular reaction. Taking his mother's hand and using it as a tool shows the beginning of some "logic of action" and recognition of the adult as an independent center of activity.

At age 4, Brian cannot yet establish objects in relation to each other; instead, they remain undifferentiated prolongations of his own actions. When placed at a table facing a toy doll and a toy chair, he shows no combinal action expected at the 10-month level (Cattell 1940). He briefly picks up the doll with one hand and touches the chair with the other, but does not bring the two objects together.

He has no concept of the passage of time, expected to develop at 2 years of age (Piaget and Inhelder [1966] 1969). This lack of age-appropriate understanding produces frustrations and occasional temper tantrums. He is limited to the observable and is stimulus-bound. For Brian, there seems to be no before and no after, nor has he developed the hypothetical attitude toward possibilities.

Brian shows severe cognitive deficits that on quantitative tests fall within the sensorimotor stage. In line with Piaget's system, Brian shows qualitative improvement in all functions between ages 5 and 7. This accords with the dramatic spurt in intelligence that seems to occur in children after age 5½ (Rimland 1968).

The following excerpts from Brian's case study represent an account of his intellectual behavior during his fifth year.

That Brian is acquiring insight into the object concept can be seen in his momentary protest at the disappearance of his mother, asking, "Carmen, where are you?" He begins to search for hidden objects of high appeal, such as books and crayons, in the closet, car trunk, or their usual places. He comes to understand the notion of hiding places but also comes to realize the permanency of objects. He knows a missing book has substance, permanence, and a location in space, and that its continued existence is independent of his actions. Brian masters the object concept of a thing "out there" and independent in existence from his own action.

He gradually begins to explore new things through action schemes with which he is familiar; he removes an obstacle to reach a desired but inaccessible object; he begins to think actively, devising plans and ideas as means to various ends.

Although Brian continues to imitate events automatically, he begins to imitate movement involving parts of his body that he cannot see, for instance, his face. He copies the act of sticking out his tongue in the presence of a model, a mongoloid child at church, and even without a model continues the same direct imitation (a sensorimotor imitation). He copies the screaming tantrum of another child in his schoolroom and threatens an imitation of throwing milk.

He begins to look at other children and laugh in imitation as if playing with them.

He actively seeks new means through differentiation of old schemata. He shows trial and error but with greater freedom of means and a better eye for what things can actually do. As he discovers new means he becomes a troublesome achiever for his mother.

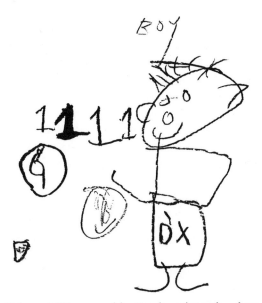

Figure 2-12. Brian, at 5½ years old, attends an intensive therapeutic hospital program and draws a normal picture—a sign of progress in his intellectual and emotional development.

Even his drawings of the human figure progress to an age appropriate, lively figure with a whole body (two squares) and a head with ears and hair. This particular drawing (Fig. 2-12) probably signals some dramatic psychophysiological reorganization. By assessing the object's character—now recognized as continuing to exist beyond the limits of the perceptual field, when it is no longer felt, seen, or heard—one can almost pinpoint a leap from the sensorimotor, prerepresentational stage to the representational or symbolic stage described by Piaget ([1936] 1952), an advance essential to Brian's further development.

Brian moves through the "terrible 2" stage at chronological age 5 years; he reaches higher and shows new initiative in pulling things to him, in opening things (he will open two bottles of soda, pour eight glasses full, and try to carry them all on a tray). Brian's mother becomes more nervous with the increase in his trial-and-error activity.

Slowly, during his fifth year, he steps toward the realization that things exist apart from his actions on them. Searching an area to find an object, he progresses to searching systematically for hidden objects, gaining a better idea of location and position in space.

He realizes that the impressions seen, heard, and felt can all belong to a single object, and that one object can be located in relation to another. The concept of physical space helps him organize himself in his environment. He recognizes and responds to the telephone ringing, whereas earlier he gave no response even when he was on top of the phone. Similarly, he begins to react to a knock at the door that heralds the sight of someone. Thus, during year 5, the concept of space develops jointly or as a by-product of Brian's object concept.

A sense of temporal order also takes hold. Through routine signals, Brian anticipates the arrival of his school bus each morning and waits by the window until it arrives, riding in a bus being one of his favorite activities. He begins to anticipate and predict time by the signal of a television image. He responds "five o'clock," "six o'clock," and so on, based on the appearance of a television screen image at the time. He especially awaits a "cue" for six o'clock and, like internal clockwork, turns the selector to his favorite television shows, "The Lottery Game" and "The Brady Bunch."

Elementary Spatial Relationships

Brian's conception of elementary spatial relationships appears normal from 3 to 7 years of age (Leiter 1969a, 1969b; Terman and Merrill 1973). His general frame of reference is perceptual rather than linguistic, and he is acutely aware of concepts involving patterns and symmetry. He readily detects a perceptual category. For example, while sitting in a play seat that swivels, he immediately turns his head to focus on an oblong, cut-out portion in the back of the seat, rather than playing in the seat itself. He recognizes geometric shapes, explores whole contours, and touches these contours. He observes progressive differentiation of shapes according to their angles and dimensions (circle and ellipse, or square and rectangle). Brian accelerates in perceptual activity from ages 3 to 7; his perceptions are active and integrated into his system of sensorimotor coordinations, binding them together. Perception acts as a steering function for him.

At age 4 years, Brian actively searches out objects that will allow his perceptual discrimination ability to function as expected at the 8- to 10-month level (Piaget and Inhelder [1948] 1956). He throws a slice of cheese in the air again and again, examines it carefully, turning it or turning his head to see it from different angles, and occasionally looking at it from varying distances. Once in a while he traces its contour.

Wake Up!

Figure 2-13. Patterns of movement resemble the brilliance of phantasmic images; the movement, animation, and scintillation effects are described in physiologically caused or drug-induced visual hallucinations. (Used by permission, Masters and Houston 1972.)

He explores the square and plays tricks focusing his eyes, as if to say, "It's new, it's new, and this is new, too." He is absorbed in perceptual mind games. Spontaneous activity of his visual system is liberated from normal inhibitions to hypnotic proportions. Moreover, his visual perceptual games closely resemble the hallucinations that may accompany a gamut of metabolic, neurological, or psychological conditions (Fig. 2-13; Mize 1980). At age 4 years, Brian finds patterns of movement, interrelationships between pattern and movement, and modes of movement change to be fantastic, captivating, wondrous.

At age 5 years, Brian delineates objects and their relationships in space as would any normal 5-year-old. His drawings rapidly develop in complexity as discovery and awareness of his environment grows. His drive for photographic representation can be seen in the photographic picture (Fig. 2-14) he paints of his living-room window, showing six window panes, an air conditioner to one side, cars lined up outside, a sun with a different type of smile, and a Goodyear blimp in the sky, which he follows by running from window to window and

Figure 2-14. Perceptual photograph of Brian's living-room window. Age, 5
     years.

adds to his drawing. He uses thick tempera paint, mixing hues of green
and blue, adding red and yellow in the window panes.

Overall, Brian, at age 6 years, is at a relatively advanced level of
shape discrimination and typically extracts from the object only that
which he is actually able to construct through his own actions. His
every perceived shape is assimilated to the schema of the coordinated
actions required to construct it. His increasingly complex pictorial
images accurately reflect the constructional process at the 7- to 8-year
level (Piaget and Inhelder [1948] 1956).

In terms of perception, Brian, at age 6 years, knows what distance
is, what constitutes a straight line or a perspective or a metric figure.
He becomes even further advanced in representing space; unfortunately, he is unable to translate this into creative expression or imagination, and his efforts are bound to direct perception. In his drawing of
a house (in file) at 6 years, 8 months, he begins with the smoke,
drawing the abstract first. He is able to relate the smoke and the house
in a correct spatial relationship without guidance from the lines of the
house that are still to be drawn. He draws smoke that shows the wind
blowing, in this case, from right to left. This indicates leftward orientation bias expressed by the degree of the smoke's deviation from an
almost direct upward course. He draws using his right hand with an
adult pencil grasp, demonstrating some pathoformicity, left to right
being the conventional direction of force. (See Levy, Meck, and

Figure 2-15. Visual realism. Age, 6 years, 10 months.

Staikoff [1978], on leftward orientation in autistic children aged 3 and 4 years.)

At 6½ years of age, Brian enters the advanced stage of intellectual realism at the 6- to 7-year level (Piaget and Inhelder [1948] 1956), drawing everything that is there, straight lines, angles, squares, and other simple geometric figures, although without exact measurements, proportions, or visual perspective. He draws a car sideways, but seems to have wanted to put in two license plates. Faced with a problem, he adapts by using the space at the side of the page extending beyond the drawn car.

He shows visual realism at the 8- to 9-year level (Piaget and Inhelder [1948] 1956), all at once taking some perspective, proportion, and distance into account. He produces accurate geometric shapes right away and develops horizontal and vertical axes. His drawing includes roads and cars, together with indications of direction, distance, and general setting. His perceptual skills develop, while his drawings show roads with Stop and One-way signs and various trucks and cars amid complicated networks of roads (Fig. 2-15).

He draws cars perpendicular to the road (in the style of one in an advanced perceptual stage) rather than lying flat on the sides of the road or arbitrarily using the road as a background. Drawing is seen to be a map organized in terms of what is important to Brian as an individual, giving a prominent or central position to his own landmarks. His graphic work shows visible thinking, and displays thrift, conservation, and principles of organization and sequence, which will become features of his problem solving.

At age 6½ years, Brian eventually comes to recognize the circle, ellipse, square, rectangle, and all the irregular shapes involving topological relationships at the 6- to 7-year level (Beery 1967a, 1967b; Piaget and Inhelder [1948] 1956). At 6 years, 9 months, in a visual-motor task (Fig. 2-16; Bender 1946) designed to diagnose brain injury, he makes characteristic errors of rotation and integration significant to the brain-injury group. (See Bender's [1938] discussion of diagnostic criteria for brain injury.) Brian's substituting lines for dots, drawing figures as lines to eliminate all the dots, is a rare and primitive response. His design shows simplification and dedifferentiation from a more complex process to a simpler one. He draws the curves in both vertical and horizontal sections as spikes, showing difficulty drawing curves. This copying task requires a high level of integrative behavior that is not necessarily specific to visual-motor functions and tends to break down with brain injury.

Brian's cognitive structure becomes more elaborate and systematized with age, and the stimulus field becomes an increasingly important determinant of his perception. His perceptions, however, are more stimulus-bound and more dependent on sensory information than the normal child's. The laws of field organization are much more compelling. He depends on sensory-perceptual properties rather than inferred conceptual manipulations, and does not move on to an appropriate deductive orientation. In the normal linguistic orientation, children, with age, subdue processing of the spatial pattern. Brian is not shifting his framework nor attending to the linguistic meaning. His behaviors are preverbal and not mediated by signs and symbols.

Lack of Abstract Attitude

Brian shows a concrete rather than abstract attitude in his intellectual development from 3 to 7 years of age. His ability to comprehend and manipulate verbal symbols and to employ classificatory schemata is poor. His perception, imagery, and ideation are all dependent on the physical presence of objects and are not moving along the concrete-abstract dimension characteristic of cognitive sophistication.

What exactly is abstract attitude? After a great deal of experience with brain-damaged patients during and following World War I,

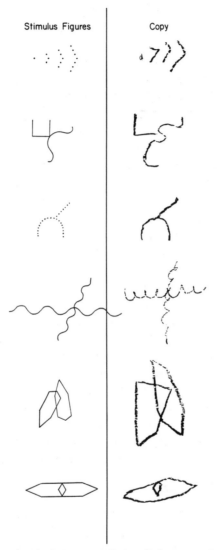

Stimulus Figures   Copy

Figure 2-16. In a visual motor gestalt test Brian, age 6 years, 9 months, substitutes lines for dots. Substituting lines for dots is of high diagnostic value in the brain-injured group (Bender 1938). He draws curves as spikes. (Used by permission, Bender 1946.)

Goldstein and Scheerer (1941) developed five tests of abstract thinking
that constitute a test battery. They believe that the main effect of brain
damage is concreteness and impairment of an abstract attitude, which
they define in terms of eight basic conscious and volitional modes of
behavior. They define abstract attitude as:

- Detaching our ego from the outer world or from inner experiences
- Assuming a mental set
- Accounting for acts to oneself; verbalizing the account
- Shifting reflectively from one aspect of the situation to another
- Holding in mind simultaneously various aspects
- Grasping the essential of a given whole; breaking up a given whole
  into parts, isolating and synthesizing these
- Abstracting common properties reflectively; forming hierarchical con-
  cepts
- Planning ahead ideationally; assuming an attitude towards the "mere
  possible" and thinking or performing symbolically. (p. 4)

Abstract attitude is conspicuous by its absence in Brian's and perhaps many autistic children's cognitive patterns. Brian understands
ideational relationships only on the basis of direct, tangible experience
of concrete imagery or from empirical exposure to numerous particular
instances of a given concept or proposition; his mental activity is,
therefore, quite limited. Spatial and temporal distances between the
elements of his visual field are small, compared with mature classification that involves representation of objects not present and unlimited
spatial and temporal distances between elements.

Brian's lack of an abstract attitude is also reflected in his general
behavior. For instance, he is initially able to perform expressive movements such as eating in appropriate situations, but is unable to demonstrate them outside the situation that demands them. He has no difficulty using a known object in a situation that requires it, but he is
totally at a loss if asked to demonstrate an object's use outside of a
concrete situation, and at a greater loss if asked to demonstrate a
function without the concrete object, i.e., pretend. At age 4 years,
Brian is able to drink milk normally out of a glass, but if given an
empty cup and asked to demonstrate how one brings the cup to the
mouth to drink (or pretend to feed a doll, 19- and 20-month level;
Cattell 1940), he is unable to do so. Nor can he imitate the action
after it has been demonstrated for him.

Brian's inability to grasp the abstract at age 4½ years impairs all of his voluntary activities. He is docile and wayward, lacking initiative and purpose and the normal strength to persist. He has great difficulty starting a performance that is not determined directly by external stimuli. Thus, at age 5, he is unable to recite a series of numbers on demand, unless his father begins the series by prompting a response, behavior typical of the completion phenomenon described in organic cases (Geschwind, Quadfasel, and Segarra 1968; Benson 1979).

Gradually, at age 5, Brian comes to show a minimal capacity for approaching things that are only imagined; that is, he begins to have the capacity to free himself from a concrete situation and turn to something already in mind, usually his drawing, writing, or reading. To quote from Brian's case study:

Brian develops a compulsive interest in numbers and letters, which seem always in mind and which he fastens on as a secure constant. Letters and numbers allow Brian inexhaustible manipulation; letters and numbers will always be somewhere.

He begins, at age 5½, to demonstrate the principle of functional assimilation, in which spelling and counting feats commence with the infantile pleasure of functional enjoyment, the *Funktionslust* described by Bühler and Hetzer (1928). Just as an organ needs nourishment in proportion to its growth and functioning, so Brian uses his cognitive structure over and over for the sheer pleasure of exercising a biological function.

He develops perceptual schemes exclusively around shape and sym-metry and uses objects to satisfy his need to function actively. His perceptual schemata eventually generalize into a variety of objects. He jumps with glee at game shows that flash numbers and letters on the television screen. He spends long hours studying catalogues, scanning books, and manipulating blocks and magnetic letters to form words.

His perceptual schemata are not passively activated by excitants; rather, Brian constantly scans and scrutinizes visual detail, searching for stimulation that will exercise his schemata. In a room typical of an office, with paper, pencils, pictures, etc., he seeks out objects, num-bers, and letters that correspond to anything in his perceptual schemata, as a hungry animal seeks food. The schemata assimilate the environmental stuff that provide the food necessary for Brian's concrete autistic thinking.

Having acquired a minimal capacity to free himself from concrete situations, Brian's perceptual interests expand, while his drawings show calendrical quantities duplicated from memory.

Brian begins, at age 5½, to show the idiot savant feature of the autistic syndrome and writes numbers with phenomenal eidetic imagery, a capacity of some children and a few adults. These individuals can examine a picture for several moments, then cast before their mind's eye an image with positive color and high detail (Haber and Haber 1964; Stromeyer and Psotka 1970). Unlike an afterimage, the eidetic image stays still while the eyes move about inspecting its details. The reality of eidetic imagery has often been questioned, for there has so far been no adequate test to distinguish between superior memory of a picture and a projected eidetic image (Traxel 1962). Eidetic imagery projection was once thought to be a normal stage in the development of all children and related to other facts of early cognitive development, such as sensory rather than verbal modes of encoding experience, and concrete rather than abstract modes of thought. However, Klüver (1965) has raised the question whether eidetic memory is a normal phenomenon with adaptive significance or whether it is essentially maladaptive and a direct manifestation of brain pathology.

Brian demonstrates his eidetic imagery and duplicates an Illinois license plate number (Fig. 2-17). The general gestalt is rectangular, similar to an actual license plate, and he writes "LAND OF LIN-OLION." His memory organization begins to stand out, in contrast to

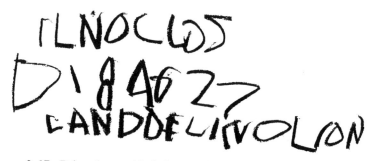

Figure 2-17. Brian shows eidetic imagery and draws a near-exact replica of a license plate. Age, 5 years, 9 months.

his inanity; still his mere organic retentiveness bears no relationship to his mental powers.

In a study of eidetic imagery among the retarded, Siipola and Hayden (1965) reported that eight out of 16 brain-injured children possess eidetic imagery, compared with only one out of 18 familial retardates. In a population of 151 normal primary school children, Haber and Haber (1964) found 12 children with eidetic memory. The incidence of eidetic imagery is, therefore, low, an estimated 8% of the normal child population.

Richardson and Cant (1970) suggest that eidetic imagery may be a normal phenomenon in most children and disappears by the time they are 7 or 8 years old. Some children may have difficulty processing visual information at higher cortical levels as a result of brain damage or an optical defect, and may continue to use the eidetic ability as a high-capacity, short-circuit memory system, but it is essentially a compensatory mechanism. Selfe (1977) attests that language becomes a shorthand for reality, and with the increasing use of language in the developing child, mental imagery is supplanted and decays through lack of use. This is in accord with the notion that eidetic imaging is age related.

Learning

From 3 to 7 years of age Brian clings tenaciously to whatever aspect he can organize into concrete sense and to those performances that lead to the experience of success and mastery. He does this because, in the absence of an abstract attitude, it is the only way he can come to terms with a world beyond his power to comprehend. He begins to show peculiar selective retention, such as unit groupings of numbers or spelling letters that will make concrete (but not abstract) sense. His task is to accumulate piecemeal data without any attempt at an explanatory hypothesis. He contents himself with the stepwise procedure of cataloging unrelated facts ad infinitum, but reproduces them only in the situation in which he learned them.

He has an affinity for repetitious spelling similar to his tenacious repetition of numbers. He spells words phonetically, but inaccurately, without hesitation. Since he never inquires into the meaning of a word, he knows the approximate spelling and pronunciation of many more words than he understands, disclosing a problem discussed by Huttenlocher and Huttenlocher (1973) in the hyperlexia syndrome. He enu-

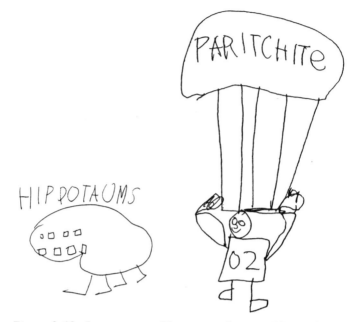

Figure 2-18. Inaccurate spelling at age 6 years, 10 months.

merates environmental objects in his drawings, e.g., "hippotaums"
and "paritchite" and, at age 6, writes his name (Fig. 2-18).

Because of the disparity between the experiences presented to him
and his level of cognitive structure, Brian learns in a very narrow
sense. One of two things happens: either he transforms experience into
a form that he can readily assimilate and consequently does not learn
what is intended, or he merely learns a specific response that will
disappear soon. In general, by age 7, he learns by association; for
example, the suggestion to go swimming elicits his getting his swimming gear.

Play

At play, Brian manipulates and lines up blocks repetitively. He rolls
a toy truck and train in and out among the blocks, around and
through, over and over, without speaking. He has no interest in toys
such as animals or a ball and, at age 4, has no conception of make-
believe games.

Through play behavior from 3 to 7 years of age, it becomes clear
that concepts for Brian are unstable yet rigid, and reality is perceived

as constantly changing impressions. Since any change is disturbing in his play, he clings to narrowly established concepts and develops compulsive behavior. His dread of change and incompleteness is a major factor in explaining his protective perseverance and limited variety in spontaneous activity.

By age 4, Brian shows none of the symbolic play expected between 18 and 24 months (Largo and Howard 1979); thus his play behavior remains consistently sensorimotor (Piaget [1936] 1952, [1937] 1954). He is a pattern maker rather than a dramatist (Wolf and Gardner 1979), dealing with object attributes instead of events. His play is characterized by (a) visual exploration—he explores objects with his eyes, fingering and turning them, and (b) spatial exploration—he engages in container play typical of a 13-month-old infant, exhibiting fill-and-empty, pull-in-and-pull-out activity (Gesell and Ilg 1943; Largo and Howard 1979). He stacks and lines up blocks, groups the same type of objects, and rolls a train and car side by side, but does not join them in relational play. He likes musical songs and claps and stomps on musical cue. He plays inappropriately with toy cars and his bicycle, immediately turning them over to repetitively rotate their wheels. His interest is in objects themselves, not in their functioning in relation to himself.

He likes primitive sensations and delights in being swung around or thrown in the air by his father. At the park, he gradually begins to swing and climb; however, he does not respond to attempts to play ball. He shows no interest in the play of other children and exhibits solitary play even when grouped closely with others.

At age 5, Brian's play behavior and other areas of development shift for the better. He shows kinds of symbolic play not present before. At age 6, he even shows game behavior and, on a rare occasion, fantasy.

He winds up a mouse toy on wheels, actively attempting to keep the mouse from running off the table's edge. He plays with the mouse and then attempts to play with the mouse and a car together, first trying to fit the mouse into the car, then putting the car on the mouse. He begins to engage in fantasy play, saying softly, "drive it," as he pushes the car.

In general, Brian's play tends toward stereotype, and he prefers quiet activities—puzzles, drawing, and filling in workbooks—over gross motor play. His play occurs exclusively in familiar situations that are free of tension or potential danger. His home is most conducive to play; he plays for many hours each day.

He develops unique tastes in play, which appear in distinct stages. He becomes fixed on one thing and repeats it until he incorporates it into the next stage. This repetition seems to give him a degree of security and mastery; he produces the same figure again and again, for example, in his drawings. Brian's play also seems largely to serve a certain escape pattern into which he can withdraw for hours at a time from an incomprehensible and overstimulating environment. Because there is a strong arousal energy in his play, he can occupy himself endlessly in solitude.

Although more catholic in his tastes than most normal children, Brian comes up with very constricted hobbies. As might a normal child, he builds constructions with his Lego blocks at year 4, lines up his cars at year 5, then becomes fascinated by trains at year 5½. He is visually very alert and draws faces of the engineer on the side of the train; he labels parts of the train ''Santa Fe'' and ''Fire Unit'' (in file) at year 5½. Next, he writes numbers and letters at year 6½ that parallel his emerging ability to read, and he draws roads and signs (Fig. 2-19) with arrows marking ''Exit'' and ''Lake Street,'' illustrating his phenomenal memory for words, numbers, and visual images.

Brian wants to read everything in sight but has little comprehension of the words. Ironically, in play, he constructs his own library of books

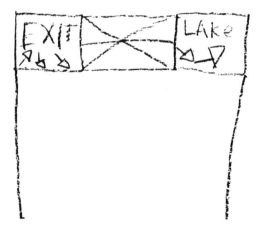

Figure 2-19. Intricate road signs seen on Brian's bus ride to school. Age, 6 years, 6 months.

in his reading and writing stage, creating "My Ball Book," "My Egg Book," "My Oil Book," and "My Puppies Book." The activity is highly structured and mimics a workbook activity; Brian includes exact guidelines on which to cut, paginate, and carries out the same instructions on his replicas. He continues this activity, as others, to the point of absolute monotony. Each of his hobbies seems an outgrowth of the previous one.

In a cut-and-paste hobby, he demonstrates a stunning flight of mental imagery. As if he may never display this activity again, in two sittings he suddenly constructs a flurry of detailed cutouts, including a truck, a unicycle, a wheelbarrow, a Goodyear blimp, an airplane, a circus truck, and many other figures, with no break in concentration. In addition, he makes his own dot-to-dot game, obviously pleased with the sheer motor aspect of drawing. In play, he draws whatever he likes and whatever comes to mind, making a game of drawing. From these activities it seems reasonable to assume that Brian's hobbies are likely to expand with awakening interests but will always be for self rather than for a social purpose.

The Drive to Self-Actualize

Brian's intellectual behavior, then, begins at age 6½ to represent a modification of concrete stages in normal development and becomes pathologically conditioned as a coping or adapting mechanism. If we assume that an organism is governed by a tendency to actualize its individual capacities as fully as possible, this can be regarded as a tendency to maintain the status quo to preserve the self. A defective organism would then be driven to an abnormal degree to exercise the functions nature permits, because these are the only performances through which he can actualize himself and come to terms with his surroundings.

If one can generalize from Brian's case study, the nature of autistic intelligence appears to utilize "preserved" intellectual capacities in the best possible way and to adapt in the best possible manner within its normal nature. (See Goldstein's [1940] discussion of adaptation of abnormal persons to defects.) From this viewpoint, we can understand intellectual behavior, or lack of it, in the autistic child. Brian's mental activity is governed by his tendency to actualize his individual capacities, his "nature," as much as possible. Thus, the primary organization of organismic functioning includes both the autistic child and his environment. We see him constantly seeking a constancy or delicate balance with his environment, a problem discussed by Goldstein (1940) in relation to the figure-ground, in which there is a continuous interplay between the biological organism and the environment that assures harmony between it and the ever-changing outside world.

In Brian's individual cognitive patterns, we can see his character. In actualizing his nature, "himself," he shows the drive toward self-actualization (Goldstein 1939). He is striving for self-preservation and trying to maintain a state of being by sparing his thinking.

He is clearly an ill organism, but he is functioning adequately for his condition, expending much psychological energy in very limited areas of cognitive development. He demonstrates Goldstein's (1940) concept of total reactivity and is compensating for the ill effects presumed to result from organic brain disease in autism. Intellectually, Brian is functioning in the best adapted manner.

DEVELOPING COMMUNICATIVE SPEECH

Brian's auditory behavior is possibly the most aberrant feature of his conduct from 3 to 7 years of age. He does not respond (or may respond erratically) to the human voice and to common sounds. He has a low tolerance for large amounts of speech directed at him, and becomes frustrated in conversational situations, becoming confused and excited, particularly if the auditory level is high.

Brian's voice is high-pitched, monotonous in tempo, and mechanical sounding. The volume is low when he speaks with strangers, loud with familiar people. He has excellent articulation at age 4, but does not use his voice projectively to communicate or attend meaningfully to the vocalizations of others, as expected at the 9-month level (Cattell 1940). His inflection pattern occasionally resembles his mother's, whose native language is Spanish.

Brian's deficient language ability is dramatically emphasized by a problem he has in producing and comprehending the spoken word. Of greater importance is his apparent lack of ability to use "inner" language for thinking and conceptualization. He is unable to give a word conventional meaning, to organize symbols and attach them to what he hears, or to store and retrieve a word or mental schema for meaningful expression, a symptom-complex that demonstrates features of Myklebust's (1954) language-disordered central aphasic.

Of high diagnostic significance, Brian, at age 4 years, is unable to compensate for his lack of verbal symbol facility by using the visual modality (as children do who are born deaf), and shows no particular visual awareness or visual understanding of his surroundings (Leiter 1969a, 1969b). A compounding factor is that at age 4 he is unable to attain meaning through nonlinguistic signs (Kubicek 1980; Riguet et al. 1981; Wing 1969) such as facial expression at the expected 7-month level, and does not understand gesture at the 9-month level (Cattell 1940). At age 4, he says a few single words at the 15-month level (Cattell 1940): "orange juice," "hot dog," "bake a cake," "banana," "apple," "raisin," "cluck, cluck, cluck." Brian identifies well-drilled picture vocabulary cards of concrete objects at the S-B III-year level (Terman and Merrill 1973) and recognizes numbers and letters.

At age 4, he names body parts at the 19- and 20-month level (Cattell 1940) and ten foods; all identifying words or labels are nouns. He is unable to point at pictures for recognition at the 17- and 18-month level (Cattell 1940) and unable to comprehend that the word *point* represents an action, not an object. He does not understand the function of objects at the 30-month level (Cattell 1940); for example, he holds a ball up to his ear.

Language as Concretion

At age 4, Brian still shows both minimal language and nonlanguage conceptual formation (Cattell 1940; Leiter 1969a, 1969b; Terman and Merrill 1973). He is at a perceptual level in Wepman's (Wepman et al. 1960) model of language function, at which stimuli are received, stored, and acted on but not given "meaning." In Wepman's model of language function, his perceptual level is modality-bound, which would be basic to conceptual activity in the normal child, except that Brian uses speech without language. He is echolalic, repeating words and phrases without meaning and word calling when reading, translating neither visual nor auditory symbol into meaning.

He miscues and associates the wrong symbol with the experience. For example, he says, "thank you" in association with giving something to someone. Again, when instructed to draw a house, he draws a birdhouse, then a doghouse, and finally the desired house (in file).

Brian's success in verbal association and rote memory, in contrast to his failure in reasoning and comprehension, call attention to how language functions in the mentally deficient. Normally, the two processes of verbal association and reasoning are interwoven, but in abnormal cases language is limited to concrete, situational speech reactions, and the person has difficulty grasping the abstract, conceptual, and symbolic level of language.

Autism and aphasia are easily cross-diagnosed because of similarities in verbal output. From a neurological construct, various degrees of comprehension and verbal production are "knocked out." As discussed in Geschwind, Quadfasel, and Segarra's (1968) neurological case of mixed transcortical aphasia, comprehension is severely affected, speech is barely produced, yet the patient can easily repeat what he hears, a function that can be carried on by the speech area itself.

Brian's deficiency may be camouflaged by two facts: (1) he produces abstract words not in their abstract meaning but in the situational sense of his concrete realism, and (2) associative memory for many speech automatisms is not supported by understanding their generic meaning and broader implications. The discrepancy between verbal association (success) and reasoning (failure) is fact, but what it signifies neurophysiologically is only now becoming known.

In the follow-up study of Brian's speech development at age 6, he is still unable to use words independent of ego-centered situations, nor can he engage in the give-and-take of conversation, reflecting his handicap in reasoning abstractly. He produces two types of speech: (1) higher ego-centered, pertaining either to action, situations, or subjective emotional experience and (2) automatic, stereotyped, associative. Brian associates all singing with that single, inflexible song, "Happy Birthday"—a situational or associative memory that ushers in an incorrect response. Brian loudly sings "Happy Birthday" at church while everyone else sings hymns. He randomly expels chains of disassociated words and phrases and whatever else comes to his mind.

The degree to which Brian uses words at age 6 without understanding them is demonstrated in the following example:

How many plants . . . jump rope . . . reindeer . . . Ah! I could have a V-8. . . . Where's your old clothes? . . . . Frrooostyyyy theee Snoooooooowmannnnnn. . . . 1, 2, 3, 4 . . . She wants to talk, slow talk, slow talk, she wants to talk. . . . Simon says . . . Tyrone, get your cup, Tyrone, I told you to get your cup. . . . I HAVE NO CASH!

He gives the impression that he is compelled to utter many remembered words and phrases, as if an automatic stimulus-response mechanism were operating (hearing a phonetic sequence, executing it motorically, connecting both responses with a situation, repeating the response when the same or a similar situation occurs). For example, reacting to his mother's accidental spilling of detergent on the floor, he scolds her, saying, "You shouldn't do that. . . . Oh, you are going to be soooooo sorry. I told you not to do that. . . . You're not going to have crackers!" Brian is reenacting a disciplinary scene in his schoolroom that day.

In another instance, Brian exclaims, "Good waiting papa! Good talking papa!" as the father is watching him look at books in the drugstore. In this example, "good waiting" and "good talking" are terms he has heard used for positive reinforcement and behavior modification at school.

Like a conditioned robot, Brian answers the telephone in a parrotlike manner without the appropriate expressive gestures and without actually waiting for an answer, saying, "Hello, how are you today, fine." Although it might appear to be a friendly, polite response, the tone is without friendliness; his friendly response seems to be the product of his mother's efforts to socialize him and his failure to grasp the propriety of these verbal responses. In another instance, teachers teach Brian to ask a question, and he will enjoy asking it endlessly. He makes a monotonous game out of "new" verbiage: "What color is this? What color is this? What color is this? What color is this?"

The above-mentioned expressions could imply generalization and conceptual meanings, but they are purely situationally determined, activated by no conscious deliberation. Their only sense might lie in the relief gained by coping with a situation through automatically rattling off linguistic associations.

Literalism in Speech

To obtain a clearer sense of autistic speech, a recording is made in Brian's apartment one afternoon after school. Brian is seated at a small wooden table in his living room, his mother seated to the right of him on a couch. Triggered by the workbook activity in front of him, and by his own spontaneous drawing, Brian displays a stream of monologue speech. He seems not to notice nor be interested in his mother and makes few attempts to communicate or interact. The following is a recorded sample of Brian's autistic speech at age 6 years, 11 months. The recording is 20 minutes long.

One little, one little Indians, four little five little six little Indians, seven little eight little nine little Indians ten little Indian girls and boys (singing).

One little two little Indians four little five little seven little eight little nine Indians, seven little Indian boys and girls.

Water please (looking to mother fleetingly).

One is the saddest one, lllll, lll ll (hums "Onward Christian Soldiers"). One, one two, one two one two three (hums "Onward Christian Soldiers").

What number, what number TWO!

That's the book with M!

Lowly worm.

Two, two, color, two, two purple.

Two, one two.

Two, two dddddd, red red red red red red redredredredredredred.

Red, red red. REDREDREDREDREDREDREDRED REDREDREDREDRED.

Three three three three and three threeeeeee e eeeeeee eeee wewewewewewewewewewewe. Three, three eeee eee, three, threeeeeee, three, two two two two.

Where's three squares? Screech, schreech, schreechchchchchchchch. Where is it, where's the square three? Where's three? Where's three? Dddd! Three. Three squares. Right here, three? Under the table. Three, three three three threethreethree, three, three, three, and eeee! Three (hums "Onward Christian Soldiers"). Three, three, three, three, three, threeee, three, three. Three, three, three three three.

Four. Four. Fourfourfourfourfour.

Eeee eeee!

WILD BILL HICKOK.

Wet and dry, wet and dry.

Four, four four and four. Fourfourfourfour! (hums "Onward Christian Soldiers"). Four, four, and four. Four is first! First! First! First! Four, four, four, fourrrfour, WHUP, aaaaaa aaaaaaaaa.

One, two, three, four, five. One, two, three four, five. (Mother asks, "What is this?") Cap. ("What is this?") Cap.

The alligator. Crow. Crow. One. Four. Eeeeee, seven, WHROOOOOOOOww. Ddd, eee, dededededeed. Whwhwhwhwh, who chchchchc. (Silence)

Home work! Home work! Home work! (Silence)

Hot dog. (Silence)

Sock. Sock. (Silence)
Tires. (Silence)
Psh, zzzz, zzzz, ZZ . . . zzzz, zzzz . . . zzzz
(Silence and end of tape.)

At the end of the recording, Brian moves to the floor, taking his drawing activity with him. He playfully creates the dot-to-dot motor game and incorporates his favorite car, a license plate, and his favorite "blimp" and other inanimate objects (a hot dog, a sock, tires, a waffle, and a truck) and labels the objects in his drawing game.

Word productivity is not a good index of language nor is it prognostically significant; we must ask what Brian comprehends. At the expected 3½-year level (Terman and Merrill 1973), when asked, "What must you do when you are thirsty?" Brian responds, "Drink." However, after a story has been read aloud (Gray and Robinson [1963], Reading Passage No. 1) and he is asked, "Who was the boy talking to?" Brian responds, "going swinging," an incorrect and inappropriate response. In general, Brian is compliant when given a direction or asked a question, although he cannot make a decision if given two choices. When given a multifaceted direction in the Stanford Binet Intelligence Scale for Children at the expected 4½-year level (Terman and Merrill 1973), Brian, at age 4 years, has difficulty following it; but he is able to follow it one direction at a time.

Brian, at age 6½ years, knows many nouns, for instance the color names; but he knows few verbs, few prepositions, and few concepts. In a simple exercise to assess concept comprehension through a non-verbal task such as drawing, he resorts to characteristic behavior, using enumerative verbalization or drawing objects. He applies this procedure indiscriminately when the task situation overtaxes his powers of adjustment and understanding. For example, he correctly shows a boy and a girl, demonstrates running, and the concept of bigger and smaller. However, when asked to show a sunny day, he simply shows the object (sun), and when asked to show a day at school, he draws a school bus.

Enumerative verbalization, therefore, is a substitute activity for normal response. It also is the chief avenue of Brian's self-expression and for establishing some positive contact with his social surroundings, especially rapport and recognition. He enjoys identifying objects outdoors and can spend hours in this activity, to his mother's complete exhaustion. He also reads everything in sight and grows fond of Mo-

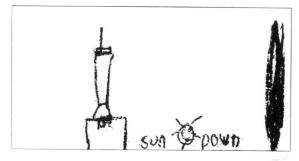

Figure 2-20. A literal understanding of "sundown." Age, 6 years, 6 months.

nopoly game cards and the game board, which entails a large amount of reading material and visual stimulation. He plays Monopoly at leisure and reads the cards, playing the game to monotony, up to four hours or more each day for two months, after which he never shows an interest in the game again. Typically, he shows an intense interest in an activity for a period of time after which his interest vanishes (but may return on some distant day).

In other games, Brian is confused and conceptually at a loss; in hide-and-seek, which he plays at his neighborhood YMCA, he is unable to grasp the meaning of the game, flaps his hands and walks on tiptoe, gazing aimlessly upward, downward, and all around, not knowing what to do, in what is for him an incomprehensible situation.

Brian learns to use "yes-no" when his father tells him that he will give him pretzels and milk if he says yes. This is a favorite food combination for Brian's father but not for Brian, and he learns to definitely say no. It takes many months before Brian detaches the word "no" from the specific situation and much longer before he is able to use "no" as a general term of disagreement and "yes" as a term of assent. The same type of literalness exists with regard to prepositions. Brian learns the word "sundown," demonstrating its meaning by drawing the sun actually on the ground (Fig. 2-20). He learns "in and out" in association with his penis, relational words apparently taught him by a well-meaning teacher during a washroom activity. The meaning of the word becomes inflexible and cannot be used with any but the originally acquired connotation.

Silence is essentially replaced with echolalia at age 6 years; that is, Brian repeats verbatim what he has heard others say. Speaking of himself, he says, "Carmen, do you want help?" "What do you want, Brian?" Personal pronouns are repeated just as he hears them, with no change to suit the altered situation. Not only the wording but even the intonation is retained. For example, when he acts in a silly fashion at the dinner table, he says "You are acting silly; you can't have anything to eat!!!" (Then he does not eat.)

Private Semantics

In summary, Brian's language, though well-articulated, is not meant for communication. In a psychogenic view, Whitehorn and Zipf (1943) remark:

> The abnormality of the autistic person lies in ignoring the other fellow; that is, it lies in his disregard of the social obligation to make only those changes which are socially acceptable in the sense that they are both understandable and serviceable in the group. Naturally, once the autistic person pursues his own linguistic and semantic paths of least effort, the result may well appear to his perplexed auditor as a disorder of meanings, or even as a disorder of association. (p. 848)

This notion that the autistic child may, at times, withhold or avoid language may bear some truth. Brian will manipulate situations to further encapsulate himself in a withdrawal process, but he can be bribed and, when he so desires, demonstrates better use of, and obedience to language. (See Lovaas [1977], for a theory of language development through behavior modification.)

Is autistic speech without meaning? It is possible to trace some of Brian's meaningless utterances to an earlier source. Though peculiar and out of place in ordinary conversation, these utterances are far from meaningless. For example, while holding a funnel and a small ball, Brian drops the ball into the funnel, bouncing the ball up and down and reciting "Bucket . . . the first number is four! Five! The first number is five!" Can we guess what Brian's action and speech are relevant to in this example? Here, Brian's speech applies to the drawings for the State Lottery, an individualized reference that is likewise expressed in his consecutive drawings of the television lottery game, the meaning of which is transferable only to the extent the listener or viewer can trace the course of the analogy. Only when their personal dynamic significance can be ascertained do Brian's nonsensical utterances have sense.

More nonsensical utterances appear while Brian and his mother are at lunch, following an upsetting first day in a new private therapeutic school. To gain a sense of what autistic thought is like, Brian's speech is recorded during the meal. The scene is a sunny and cool autumn afternoon: Brian's mother and he sit in a booth next to a window looking out on a major street. Brian accompanies his mother to the salad bar and helps himself to a good portion of salads and relishes. He sits down to eat, gulping the food as though he is very hungry. A steak with potatoes is served to each of them; Brian begins to play with his food and has difficulty finishing it. During the meal, he directs no comments to others, nor does he seem particularly aware of or interested in his mother's presence.

Brian's mother monitors his eating, encourages him to eat a little more, and helps him cut his meat. He passively listens and watches her. She gives him a pad of paper and pen to occupy himself toward the end of the meal, and he draws a picture. Meanwhile, his mother finishes her lunch. Brian gazes out of the window into the street, fleetingly looks around the restaurant, draws on the tablet provided, and utters sporadic disassociated sounds to no one in particular, occasionally naming things that he is drawing at his mother's request. Brian's stream of speech and drawing becomes especially dissociated, deteriorating under the increased strain of the long lunch and confinement of the booth. He makes no attempt to get up but loses interest in his drawing activity, squirms in the booth, grabs his mother around the neck while looking about the restaurant, and begins to utter unintelligible noises until they leave. Then Brian walks in front of his mother as though knowing his whereabouts. He is relaxed and swings his arms. His mother fears that he will go into the street and calls him back, takes his hand, and leads him to the parking area.

The following is a stream of autistic speech from the tape recording while in the restaurant. It shows a flight of associations and chain of nonsensical utterances. Brian is 6 years, 11 months at the time. The length of the recording is 60 minutes.

Toot toot toot toot.
(Silence)
Volvo.
(Silence)
Carmen, Carmen, Carrr . . . men, Carrrrr . . . men.
(Silence)

Uh, uh!
(Silence)
Help.
(Silence)
Good taste.
(Taking a bite of food.)
(Silence)
Hmmmm hmmm.
(Silence)
Crash car, Bsh, bsh, bsh, bsh, bsh.
(Silence)
Dee de de de de.
Ding dong ding dong. Carmen huh.
(Silence)
Breakfast. Snack. Snack.
(Silence)
Going for a ride on the truck truck truck.
Heinz, Heinz 57 sauce.
(Silence)
(Brian is requested to draw himself.)
Glasses.
(Silence)
Pee pee (goes with mother to the washroom and returns).
Shiny. Salt, salt paint the picture (lifting the salt shaker).
Salt paint the picture, paint the picture.
(Silence)
Rocket. Fefefefe. Flute, flute (playing pen like a flute).
(Silence, end of tape)

When we consider the two types of speech mechanisms, ego-centered speech and situational speech reactions, apparent inconsistencies in Brian's verbal performances become understandable. At age 6 years, Brian calls out words and sentences, but we get hints of the consequences of such a meaning deficit for Brian's social and world orientation. He cannot possibly wonder about an event because any idea of cause and effect is out of his reach. He reproduces conventional phrases like a well-conditioned automaton with an empty facial expression. The inability to adequately register and absorb human relations and social facts coincides here with Brian's impaired sense of verbal meaning. He can neither comprehend nor create complex symbolic

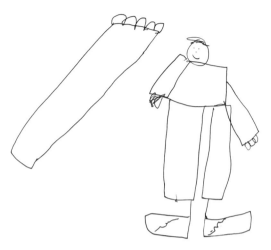

Figure 2-21. Brian, age 7 years, has difficulty acquiring and integrating concepts and at times makes painful attempts to achieve a task. Here he traces his own arm before adding two arms to his previously armless drawing.

relations. This may explain and reconcile other discrepancies in his verbal achievements.

Typically, Brian's drawings of human figures have no arms, until I press him to include arms, provoking in him a silent, painful struggle. As though to acquire the concept, he first traces his own arm next to the armless figure (Fig. 2-21). Only after enormous effort of concentration does Brian add two arms to his poorly integrated and neckless figure drawing.

3

Affect and Autism

Most of us have wondered exactly when the autistic child's uniqueness starts and whether or not mothers sense a difference as early as infancy. Unfortunately, mothers often do not recollect their autistic child's infancy well enough to provide definitive answers. This was demonstrated in the case of Brian when, two years after diagnosis and in a calmer moment, his mother was asked whether he had been limp as an infant. Brian's mother was reminded of her initial interview when she had described Brian as always having been limp when picked up in infancy. Questions were phrased so as not to refer to Brian's traits but to his behavior, his reactions to feeding, bathing, and other concrete events. With probing and by reexamining their recollections, both Brian's mother and father, when approached individually and together, were of the same opinion: that Brian, in fact, gave no clue of his infant autism. Moreover, he seemed a "normal kid." However, they thought there was a definite turning point after the first year, when slow speech development heralded manneristic behavior, leading them to suspect a problem.

EARLY ATTACHMENTS

In an attempt to learn what characterizes the autistic infant's personality, and when and how such characteristics begin, I offer the following reconstruction of Brian's early infancy:

Brian is a pleasant, passive, sweet baby, who seems always content, seldom cries, and shows positive affect. He plays quietly in his crib, and generally goes to sleep easily. There is little fussing. His times of sleep are regular, and he moves quickly into an apparently deep sleep with little motion. There is such a degree of quiescence the mother looks in on him to see if he is still breathing.

He makes a reaching-out gesture and specific postural adjustments to his mother's holding, remaining still when picked up. He moves little but appears to be very observant. He shows no active rejection of social contacts, but neither is he a cuddler. He has the emotional feel of a normal infant. The father notices real eye-to-eye contact one day as Brian suddenly looks up, stares strongly into his father's face as though looking with complete fascination.

He is interested in a flower and examines his surroundings. He mouths toys, and attempts to clap his hands in the game, pat-a-cake.

He is really loved. Mother is his companion, and she keeps him busy all day long. He plays and splashes in his bath and wading pool and smiles with excited tone to everyone.

As an infant he shows radiant and joyful behavior—quite asymptomatic.

In searching for early signs of autistic personality in the infancy period, two notions emerge. First, perhaps there is no "infantile" autism. We cannot identify signs of an autistic personality in early infancy as readily as we can the unmistakable signs evident with age. Second, because the number and variety of possible behaviors increase dramatically after early infancy, it may be difficult to demonstrate that the behavior of older autistic children always has an antecedent infant behavior. The most we can probably say is that the individual temperaments of autistic infants are the same as those of normal nonautistic infants and appear as innate tendencies that adapt in certain ways to the stimuli of their environment.

In a hypothetical sampling of autistic infants, we would likely find that an autistic infant can be very active, vigorous, intense, and easily aroused, or passive, inactive, tractable, and mild-mannered. Similarly, in a hypothetical spectrum of autistic children, parents would likely report (by a higher percentage) difficult babies, irregular sleeping and eating patterns, and more than an average amount of upset or frustration over new situations. The remainder of the mothers would likely report smooth care-giving—"happy" babies, positive in mood. The point is that the same spectrum of individual differences that occurs in normal infants is likely to occur even within the autistic population.

Since autistic infants differ, and certain characteristics are after age

1, systematically associated with membership in the autistic group, perhaps something in their early experience or genetic background will help us understand how these common characteristics arise.

Although human personality is based on individual differences, it also requires some commonality in the central issues of biological life. What are the basic adaptive issues for developing infants? Willemsen (1979) cites four that are reflected in theoretical writings on infancy:

> First, infants face the task of establishing biological rhythms—those of sleep, eating, respiration, arousal, activity, and so forth. Second, infants need some basic skills for dealing with the potentially overwhelming influx of information (stimulation) from their environments. Third, as babies react to this stimulation from the environment, they must establish some voluntary control over their own activity. Fourth, they need to practice and refine the adaptive skills they are acquiring. (p. 237)

Since babies react to these basic experiences, but in different ways, we can think of their emerging individuality as a product of their various approaches to experience.

Fear of Strangers

Looking at the relation between these common experiences and differences emerging in Brian after age 18 months, one could see fear developing in him in response to stimulation. Attempting to explain the infant's fear of strangers, Spitz (1950) names the phenomenon "eight-months' anxiety" (fear of strangers in the second half-year of life). Anxiety implies a subjective source of pain, attributed by Spitz to the infant's insight that other people are not mother—a sort of anticipatory separation anxiety—in contrast to fear, which implies an external source of pain related to the flight response of lower animals. It is of major importance to distinguish between the two factors involved, fear being an innate phylogenetically inherited reaction, anxiety being firmly connected with object relations. Other explanations, such as Freedman's (1961), discuss the undeniable fact that the stranger qua stranger is perceived as dangerous, and Jersild (1954) notes that the first fears of human infancy are spontaneous in the sense that avoidance is not built up by an association with a more primitive fear. In the ethological approach to the phenomenon of fear, Freedman (1961) suggests that infant fear may be a homologue of the apparently innate flight response found in a great majority of animal species, thus extending Spitz's cognitive-psychoanalytic interpretation and probably inaccurate term "eight-months' anxiety."

Hebb and Riesen (1943), motivational theorists, report that stimulation from the environment increases the organism's general arousal level. They consider fear to be innate and aroused when there is so much stimulation to be dealt with, it cannot be dealt with at all. That fear involves an innate factor helps explain Brian's and other autistic children's intense fear response to strangers long before they actually develop the concept of an object and a specific subjective attachment.

Stimulation Withdrawal

Korner's (1971) contention is that the underlying characteristic of an infant's individuality is the ability to take in and integrate sensory stimuli. A very active baby tends to process stimuli quickly, while a less active baby processes stimuli more slowly. Although this view has not been proved, it is known that all infants have some method for handling stimulus overload. Some cry; most fall asleep. In an environment full of massive stimulation, we see that Brian handles stimulus overload in his early infancy by falling asleep.

As he ages, Brian begins to cope with stimulation in a way common to autistic children. He shuts out stimulation by withdrawing, averting his gaze, and initiating an isolating behavior pattern. In keeping with Hebb and Riesen's (1943) view of fear, Brian's intense avoidance prevents the fear response. Fear may well be present in such an overwhelming degree (i.e., fear hypertrophy) that intense withdrawal results as a protective mechanism; as though armoring himself, Brian takes flight from stimulation. An unfamiliar situation (a form of social stress) evokes intensified fear that later dominates and suppresses much of his social and exploratory behavior. In other words, Brian appears even more autistic in "strange" surroundings. As he gets older, at year 5, and object relations begin tenuously to develop, he does not show the stranger response to members of his family, but to outsiders, as they begin to interact with him.

Common to autistic children is their way of coping with the potentially overwhelming influx of environmental stimulation, which engenders an intense fear response and withdrawal. Hypothetically, autistic children are abnormally sensitive to stimulation and likely to be in a constant state of hyperstimulation correlated with stereotyped behavior that shields them from extra stimulation. The more complex the environment, the more accentuated is the autistic behavior.

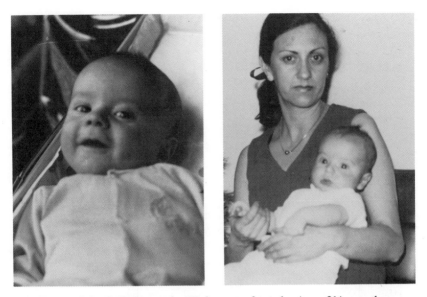

Figure 3-1. Left, in touch. *Right,* out of touch. Age, 3½ months.

In a group of autistic children, then, we would likely find a hierar-chy of symptoms indicating stress, and there would likely always be symptoms even in a 100% compatible environment, but fewer of them. Whether such an interpretation is valid depends on the nature of unre-ported data concerning stimulation. The difficulty in determining a causal relationship between stress and autistic symptoms is that it is not easy to manipulate stimulation experimentally.

Figure 3-1 demonstrates self-protection against overstimulation through a certain emotional expression. Brian's eyes show an in-touch look when he is related to his surroundings, in contrast to the usual vacant look of early infancy when he is out of touch with his surround-ings and overstimulated. Brian is navigating between states of con-sciousness as a means of managing stress. Figure 3-2 shows a "flash-light" affect from the shock of overstimulation.

In infant research, Benjamin (1963) refers to Freud's ([1900] 1953, [1920] 1955a, [1936] 1959) speculation (the *low level* theory) that a passive mechanism exists in the very young infant, a barrier that pro-tects the infant from overstimulation. Freedman (1974) emphasizes adaptive responses already present at birth, including the ability to shut out excessive stimulation, observing that the infant simply drifts into a state of sleep. Osofsky (1979) reports that most studies find that infant behavior is heavily influenced by the physiological context within

Figure 3-2. Condition of overstimulation leads to "flashlight" affect. The picture shows Brian's interest in letters—all of which are accurately positioned except "F." Age, 2 years, 2 months.

which stimulation occurs. Such factors include the individual's enduring characteristics or temperament and the transient state of arousal. While these factors remain important, they become subordinated to other principles of development, and physiological prototypes of behavioral organization give way to psychophysiological processes including anticipation, memory, and intentionality. Quantity of stimulation will always remain important, but by the third month, sustaining attention and following changes in stimulation also involve the infant's psychologically processing the content (recognition) of the stimulation. Said simply, the meaning the event has for the infant dominates its mere stimulation. Wolff (1963) points out that the infant begins to respond more selectively to stimulation, gradually moving from an organismic physiological state to a psychological one, where the competition between internal visceral stimuli and external peremptory stimuli changes to competition between an external stimulus and an internal directing factor that may be related to later attention and intentional behavior.

From another viewpoint, Tennes et al. (1972) refer to a period of absolute nonresponsivity in infant neural development during which infants are relatively invulnerable to external stimulation due to a

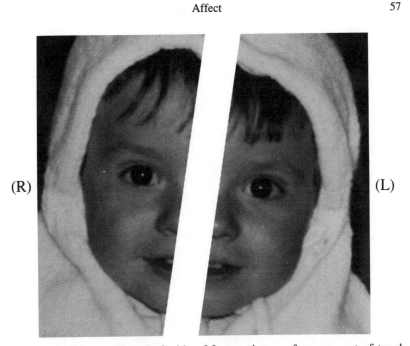

(R)   (L)

Figure 3-3. Face-reading. Left side of face registers a faraway, out-of-touch
look; the right side shows a happy, pleased, in-touch look. Age,
2 years, 2 months.

passive stimulus barrier. This is followed by a period of turning toward
the environment, when the infant is relatively vulnerable, open to
stimulation and has only preadapted tension-modulation devices for
reducing the impact of excessive stimulation.[1] Tension-modulation
devices include the beginning of coordinated attention, motor activity,
social smiling, and cooing, which mark the end of obligatory attention
and the beginning of an organized response to stimulation and a relatively more integrated means of processing it.

Again, the first signs of autism involve the head and eyes, and it is
intriguing to continue to examine the management of stimulation by
face reading (Ekman and Friesen 1975; Trotter 1983), where we view
the two sides of the autistic face separately (Fig. 3-3). The right side of
Brian's face appears to be more expressive of affect than the left side.
His face appears consistently to register a far-away, out-of-touch look
on the left versus an in-touch and happy, pleased look on the right,
possibly reflecting a state of mixed or unbalanced affect and borderline
(in-and-out) contact with his environment. Although this hypothesis
has not been proved, the right side of the face in this study sample

appears consistently to reveal more affect than the left and possibly reflects a left-hemisphere dominance.

In a discussion of stimulation, age-related changes become important. Autistic symptoms, difficult to detect in infancy, appear obvious after the first year, and may be linked to sensitivity changes in relation to stimulation, and to a psychological (cognitive) factor that in infancy takes precedence over physiological processes.

This notion of age-related changes with respect to stimulation is both an exciting and frustrating one because there are few studies of sensitivity changes between the first few days of life and the time for rich and demanding differentiation—near the end of the first year of life, a critical period requiring much coping. There is evidence in Brian's case that he responds to stimulation, but how and why does the response change? Hypothetically, physiological prototypes of behavioral organization give way to psychophysiological processes as cognition fails to "clock in" or become involved at some critical period, and a condition of hyperstimulation occurs whereby depression of affect and protective withdrawal appear adaptive as secondary consequences in the autism syndrome.

Affect in autistic infants has not been as thoroughly studied as has cognition, perception, and social behavior. Frequently, conceptual confusion in these areas has resulted from explanatory attempts divorced from consideration of the autistic infant as a complex emotional being. The development of affect is a function of the interaction of organism and environment. Biological nature sets up a core of experiences before birth, and the autistic child's uniqueness may be a way of reacting to a common experience, stemming from social experiences as well as biological bases.

Surviving Environmental Stress

Goldfarb (1964) has postulated that "each psychotic child's aberrations are seen as highly unique strategies on their part—always an adaptive response to intrapsychic and interactional processes—and oftentimes most feasibly studied on a case basis" (p. 621). This statement also applies to autistic children. Intense withdrawal in the autistic child may be regarded as adaptive and one of a series of alternative, consecutive, or coexistent survival skills through which he seeks to adjust and efficiently function as a human organism, coming to terms with his environment.

In Meyer's (1957) psychiatric approach, an autistic child may be considered a reactive type, but unlike many brain-injured people who suffer from severe anxiety or emotional lability, the autistic child reacts psychotically, not neurotically, in response to environmental stress. The autistic child's special vulnerability to environmental stress drives him to protective reactions that have survival and adaptive value, the most extreme of which is intense withdrawal. Altering one's state of consciousness is, in fact, a survival skill useful in coping with the physiological and psychological effects of stress. (See Bell's [1980] discussion of states of consciousness and [1982] thesis on intrapsychic survival skills.)

At age 4 years, Brian does not look at his mother or father and walks past them, moving farther away from them. His emotional tone is unrelated to the situation, although he is cooperative and amenable. He is responding to stimulation with a decreased range of positive and negative affect expression, with less response to environmental events, and less promptness in mobilizing a response.

He shows no interest in other children and will not play with a ball or engage in peek-a-boo. He displays emotional indifference, little or no expression of intensity or personal involvement, and an impassive facial expression. All seem to be strangers; the comings and goings of mother and father are unnoticed.

Engel and Schmale (1972) describe a condition similar to autistic withdrawal, namely conversion-withdrawal, in medical and surgical patients in whom there is a self-limited type of biologically determined withdrawal that protects the organism against excessive stimulation, acting as a primary regulatory process of organismic homeostasis. Projective psychological testing shows an emotionally responsive patient who is readily disorganized by the environment and uses withdrawal and inhibition in the service of coping (Lovitt and Weiner 1980). Withdrawal temporarily supports survival by conserving resources through disengagement and inactivity until external and internal conditions improve. It abates when the perceived overwhelming danger diminishes (similar to the waning of withdrawal in autistic children at about 5½ years when internal conditions improve through maturation, and cognitive control over affect occurs). This withdrawal occurs in other species at times of inescapable danger, and is called *tonic immobility* or *animal hypnosis* (Gallup and Maser 1977).

If the autistic child has a low threshold of sensitivity (Bergman and Escalona 1949), then most interactive contacts with the environment will be so irritating and painful that he will block off (as in the habituation phenomenon) such contact through withdrawal and avoidant behavior.

Brian displays extreme social withdrawal and isolation, now actively rejecting auditory and tactile social contacts. Mother tickles him and he responds. When he is asked a question, he makes no eye contact and gives no response. Brian appears deaf, not responding to the telephone or a fire engine siren. He does not make his wants known by any form of communicative speech or gesture.

Faced with environmental stress, the autistic child may deal with it by one or more of the following four methods: tentative and usually abortive efforts to cope, attempts to control environmental change by imposing rituals, distortion of his surroundings, or withdrawal. In his efforts to cope, he may try to avoid stress by controlling unpredictable factors in his surroundings through rituals, perseveration, and by preventing any form of variation. If these efforts fail, he may try to make the environment acceptable through distortion, fantasy, delusion, or hallucination. In children with severe autism, the environment no longer directs their thoughts. Severely autistic children appear to have little comprehension of their environment and still less information from which to derive fantasies. If none of these mechanisms succeeds in protecting the child from irritating or excessive stimulation, his only recourse is to withdraw or flee the situation.

During such avoidance behavior Brian would fall but not cry, seeming not to feel pain. He may indeed be oblivious to pain, as a highly sensitive mystic may be while in a state of spiritual exaltation, or a soldier in the excitement of battle. Deep meditation or prolonged, intense focusing of attention on inner feelings, thoughts, or images may produce a state similar to hypnotic analgesia. Indian fakirs have been observed to walk across beds of hot coals or to lie on a bed of nails or cactus thorns without evidence of pain. This human ability voluntarily to direct attention toward inner feelings, thoughts, or images, and to block out all extraneous environmental stimuli, may also explain the autistic child's ability to produce pain anesthesia.

When an autistic child is in a severely withdrawn state and one touches him to attract attention, it may evoke no response whatever. This does not mean he has lost the sense of touch; for he makes use of his tactile sense in manipulating familiar objects. His failure to respond to painful stimuli may be a form of dissociation from this kind of stimulus. He may voluntarily keep the brain sensitivity threshold minimal in defiance of stimulation from the outer world. (Presumably this is what happens under hypnotic suggestion, when for therapeutic purposes a susceptible patient can effectively exclude various sensory stimuli, especially pain.)

It has been found that sensibility to pain develops with intelligence (Melzack 1973). By pain is meant both the understanding of a localized sensation and appreciation of its intensity and the psychic reverberations of pain, the ideas and emotions it provokes that increase its magnitude. Initially these overtones may be absent, but they are important factors in the autistic child's response or lack of response to pain.

Thus in the autistic child's dissociation, we have the mechanism not only of failure to respond to pain stimuli, but also withdrawal, the essential characteristic of the autistic syndrome. The autistic child can withdraw from or dissociate sound, sight, odor, pain, and touch; just as he can withdraw from people, he can withdraw from speaking, reading, and learning. The withdrawal may be selective, partially selective, dissociative, or just simply cut off.

Where withdrawal is only partial or selective, the autistic child may acquire a highly developed skill such as drawing or working calculus problems. In such cases, the least impaired function becomes a coping mechanism used in adapting the total personality to the environment. The skill becomes the single link between the child and the adult autistic and the outer world when he is not in a withdrawn state.

LOCATING AFFECT

Spitz (1959) has been one of the most influential voices in research, for his study of infancy behavior and first social attachment. Spitz suggests three qualitative turning points in early development, each marked by a change in affectivity and each reflecting (1) a basic transformation in psychological life, (2) the emergence of new functions, and (3) a qualitatively different process for interaction with the environment.

According to Spitz, the infant's first psychological organizer is marked by the *social smile,* which represents the infant's basic distinction between the "in here" and the "out there." It signals the beginning of recognizing repeatability in the environment and awareness that will develop into anticipation. It also marks familiarity, which reflects a first emotion and relation between the infant and the environment. The new sensitivity to reliability in the environment moves development forward rapidly until the press of development forces another reorganization, viewed by Spitz as recognition memory leading to recall memory, object permanency, and other cognitive-motivational advances. Experience becomes more organized as current and previous events can be related and as events engage with expectations.

In the first year, the infant acts with regard to objects not visually present, affectively responds to their loss and recovery, and experiences affective reactions in connection with events. In Spitz's view, this reorganization is signaled by the second organizer, *stranger anxiety,* and the failure of the stranger's face to match the stored image of the mother. Spitz's third developmental organizer is supported by changes in the cognitive domain, the transition from sensorimotor behavior to representational thought and, at approximately 18 months, the beginning of verbal symbols.

Using Spitz's developmental organizers as guideposts and examining Brian's infant affect development, we see failure in all three turning points. According to Spitz's system, Brian is already psychologically disorganized in his environment by the first year, and failing to make the appropriate qualitative turning points in his development of affect. In fact, his stimulus-response behavior seems to fit a discharge, hydraulic, or homeostatic model, in contrast to normal infant development where seeking and maintaining contact with stimulation becomes prominent.

In terms of infant affect development, Brian appears to have poor psychological organization. Moreover, he appears psychologically disorganized at a critical period, when normal infants are known to be vulnerable to stimulation and when cognitive control of affect begins. He shows in infancy a poor capacity for appropriate interpersonal responsiveness and intellectual comprehension.

It would seem less a coincidence and more a predictable fate that not until after the first year does Brian show pathological behavioral change and turn away from stimulation, becoming incapable of seeking, maintaining, controlling, and tolerating contact with stimulation.

Affect Mobilization and Control

The question of affect is basic to the investigation of autistic personality. Are we discussing a state of affectlessness or a situation in which some control mechanism of affect expression has gone awry?

Alertness and affect in the autistic child diminish as contact with the outside world diminishes and autistic withdrawal increases. The observation "Brian does not have a fully fledged smile any more," from the case study at age 3, indicates his increased withdrawal.

Affect is difficult to mobilize and motivate in the autistic child,[2] although certain sensory responses—hunger, thirst, and cold—can alert him to the presence of the environment. In regard to physical stimuli the autistic child has little sense of danger and does not show typical fears. Rather, his fears originate from shock reactions to sudden stimuli in situations whose broader meaning he cannot understand. This results in the physiological coupling of an emotional shock and a disturbing event, giving rise to affect. In other words, a strong stimulus may produce affect in the autistic child in the absence of an adequate cognitive response.

At 5 years, 6 months, thunder and lightning arouse terror in Brian. He becomes very upset, puts his fingers in his ears, runs into the closet, or to his parents' bed, and must be held to be soothed. The loud noise appears to have a primitive disrupting action, not dependent on any previous experience.

The autistic child may also show more affect in situations that hold high arousal energy. For example, perceptual excitement, especially numbers, holds certain and high-arousal energy for Brian.

At 4 years, 1 month, Brian is temporarily alerted to his environment as he stands excitedly beating the air and flapping his limbs in front of a digital clock (Figs. 3-4 and 3-5). He shows surprise at the captivating numbers "popping up" unexpectedly on the digital clock in front of him, accompanied by heightened consciousness of this stimulus at the expense of other stimuli.

Autistic flapping, although obviously bizarre, may become more understandable when compared with the similar behavior of a 4- or 5-month-old infant who responds with a global reaction of pleasure to perceptual stimulation. The young infant babbles, arches himself, beats the air with his arms and moves his legs, whereas the autistic child flaps his hands. Both show affect expression limited to undifferentiated excitement in response to an intense or prolonged stimulus.

In free drawing (see Fig. 2-8), Brian, at age 6 years, 11 months, brings about his own affect in a self-stimulating activity. His drawing shows "thrilling" numbers that increase in size and give rise to and

Figure 3-4. Flapping. Brian readies himself to flap in a moment of excitement over numbers popping up on a digital clock in front of him. Age, 4 years, 1 month.

expand with affect that is not well controlled. The numbers also have resonance and a coming alive quality about them.

An autistic child may emerge temporarily and partially from his withdrawal if an extremely exciting atmosphere can be produced.

Brian, at age 4 years, likes roughhouse play and acrobatics, but otherwise he sits quietly and repetitively rotates the wheels of his toy cars.

Figure 3-5. Brian begins flapping his arms in excitement, a response similar to a young infant's global, pleasurable reaction to stimulation. Age, 4 years, 1 month.

An autistic child may also respond with affect to certain events having some element of surprise and incongruity.

Slapstick comedy elicits affect in Brian at age 5½ years, as he watches "The Three Stooges" on television and laughs as he sees people shoot water at each other.

Slapstick humor is known to be an especially strong impetus for arousing affect in children. D. G. Freedman (per. com. 30 July 1984) observed a group of young Australian aboriginal children watching slapstick comedy in a movie theater. While Australian aboriginal children as a cultural group have been found to show a nonexcitable disposition (Freedman 1974), during a slapstick movie this impassive group was brought to loud laughter.

In Brian, affect is stirred by arousing him from withdrawal to his favorite hobbies, drawing and spelling. He becomes angry when his isolation is encroached on and he is pressed to respond to a task not of his choosing. Eventually, he draws Figure 3-6. Under the increased strain of attending, he loses control and shows anger. The progression of affect is expressed in his drawing as the drawing increases in size with a sharp, barely controlled anger.

The problem of mobilizing and controlling affect is reflected in Brian's drawing of the human figure. He is instructed once again to draw a man with arms, an especially difficult task for him. Unwillingly, he draws a human figure (Fig. 3-7) without facial features and scribbled hair that suggests some emotional communication. Rather than getting up and resisting the difficult task, he leaves out details in his drawing, yet includes cars as though personalizing the drawing with one favorite object. The cars appear to coincide with the beginning of his whimsical "rrr" verbalizations.

Affect is, in fact, present but difficult to mobilize as adaptive psychopathology or withdrawal develops with excessive stress. Thus the problem of affect in autism does not represent an accidental chaotic play of excitation, but demonstrates that behind the external chaos it is possible to discover constant patterns.

From an analysis of affect in autism, three points become evident. (1) It seems highly probable that these children have a low sensitivity threshold to environmental contact and that intense withdrawal is a protective mechanism against intolerable stimulation (or hyperstimulation) that results in depression of affect. (2) When autistic children

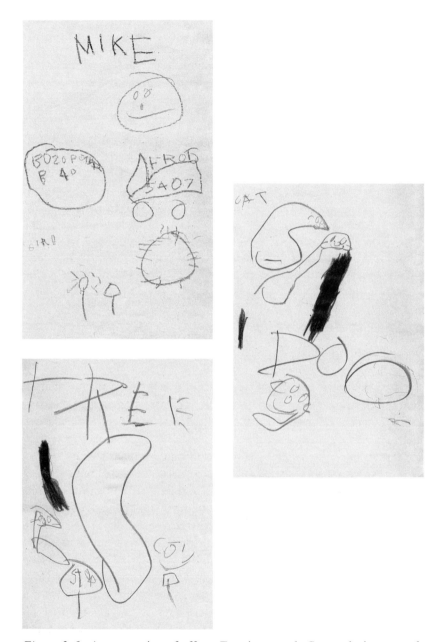

Figure 3-6. A progression of affect. *Top,* in control. *Center,* losing control. *Bottom,* out of control. Age, 5 years, 9 months.

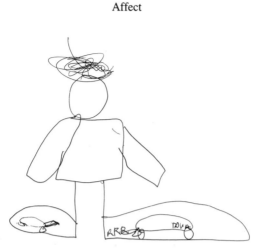

Figure 3-7. Human-figure drawing. Brian deals with anger in an original manner: he draws a depersonalized human figure with no facial features and draws feet that become a scene in themselves. Age, 6 years, 10 months.

withdraw, only intense stimuli and high-arousal energy can alert them to the environment. (3) Affect is dormant and the withdrawal process prevents its mobilization.

Again, we see that high-arousal energy situations may propel the autistic child from an intensely withdrawn state. Although arousal may be associated with the withdrawal process, affect is a more basic concern.

My premise is that withdrawal, the major protective mechanism, may obscure the core problems in autism and make the assessment of affect development difficult. Some authors (Ekstein and Friedman 1974; King 1975; Massie 1978) have suggested that although social withdrawal in the autistic child may differ in kind from that in the general population, such withdrawal, however caused, is the basic handicap. This seems plausible in that impaired relationships and social communications are certainly a cardinal feature of autism. However, social withdrawal in autism is also one of the first behaviors to improve, and some autistic children cease to withdraw in adult life (Rutter 1970; Rutter, Greenfield, and Lockyer 1967). That even after the autistic child ceases to be withdrawn, he may still remain retarded in language, have a low IQ, and show obsessive symptoms and depressed affect, argues strongly against social withdrawal being the sole cause of the other handicaps (Rutter 1968).

Affective-Cognitive Symbiosis

The findings reported thus far point to an interdependence between intelligence and affect in autism. But precisely what role does intelligence play in the development of affect?

Aholism is a cognitive process peculiar to the autistic child wherein a part assumes supremacy over the whole; it is frequently referred to as a problem in part–whole relationships. The autistic child responds to only a part of what is normally a whole perception or conception. Freud ([1913] 1955b) described an intellectual function in us that demands integration, connection, and intelligibility from anything that comes within its grasp, whether a perception or a thought. Freud hypothesized that in aholism the process of active concretion is arrested at a primitive level, leading to feelings of confusion and fear, such as we observe in the autistic child. At times nothing can intrude upon him, and nothing can comfort him. He cannot react emotionally in a satisfactory way, and attaches definite feelings to situations in which he fails to appreciate the cognitive essentials. In other words, he may grasp only a part of a situation or object because only that part could be grasped concretely.

At age 5½ years, Brian suddenly sobs relentlessly after dinner and repeats, "no papers for Brian, poooorrrr boy." He is hurt because he was not permitted to bring papers home from school. He cannot be soothed this time; the situation seems unintelligible and he cries into the next day.

In autism, a reaction seems inappropriate to us because we regard the whole situation and not merely a part. However, if we consider the autistic child's behavior from the standpoint of affective-cognitive symbiosis, we see that in the situation as it is experienced by him, his feelings may not be abnormal.

To an integrated organism, the whole setting of the stimulus and the whole state of the organism determine the pattern of response. (See Bender's [1938] discussion of the principle of the gestalt function.) Following this premise, we can use the given stimulating constellation in more or less similar settings and study the gestalt function in the pathological integrative condition. This is how the gestalt function may appear in autism.

Severe distortion of the autistic child's object relations distort his perception of people. The autistic child sees people as a conglomeration of unrelated parts, he reacts only to separate stimuli and is completely unable to see another person as a whole being apart from himself.

Brian's behavior is consistent with his perception and reflected in his first drawing of the human figure (see Fig. 2-6) as disintegrated "parts" separate from a whole.

The autistic child fails to achieve a sense of self, develops distortions of body image and anomalies of perception that indicate a deficit in gestalt function and early developmental arrest. The young autistic child is devoid of perceptual focus and lives in an environment without boundary or structure.

It seems reasonable to assume that parallels exist between affective and cognitive stages of development in the autistic child, and that gradual modification of typical autistic symptoms, from marked autism in early childhood to paranormal behavior in middle childhood, can be evaluated in terms of maturation. Hypothetically, a normal reduction in uncontrolled fear and protective withdrawal takes place in autistic children somewhere around age 6 years, when the cognitive and affective aspects of personality are again reorganized through maturation. The theory that affect seems modulated by cognitive events as well as by internal variables may be best tested by studying autistic cases in which the dynamics and consequences of this modification are present in the extreme.

Brian, at age 6, is less docile, less withdrawn, and less obsessional. A stranger enters his home; Brian still is shy and runs to bury his head in the couch. He covers his eyes with his forearm when spoken to, trying to withdraw by looking away. But mother is present and the withdrawal behavior passes.

Brian is extremely sensitive and fearful of approach by strange people, especially when the total situation is unfamiliar. But now the range of situations that frighten him seem fewer, and his fears are giving way to acceptance.

A new situation still arouses intense fear, but acceptance comes when Brian is able to cope. His emotional attitude is more accepting; he accepts more foods, even chocolate, and is a good eater. He shows more affect and screams when he hurts his head. He seems to like

Figure 3-8. At 6½ years old, while attending a neighborhood nursery school
with normal children, Brian becomes less withdrawn and makes
an effort to experience, show, and control feelings.

animals, although he is shy and careful with a neighbor's cat and dog.
He uses body gestures toward his aunt's cat.

Brian's temperament continues to be submissive compared with that
of a difficult child. He has no aggressive behavior. When a large,
impulsive boy in Brian's classroom threatens attack, Brian moves
away defenseless, yet he frequently refers to the boy punitively in his
echolalic speech at home.

The sixth year of autistic life marks a transition as the typical manifestations of autism are gradually modified. Brian adjusts in what is for
him the best adapted manner, sometimes showing a facade of nor-
malcy, but there is nothing behind the facade.

Brian notices affect in others. In picture books he looks for happy
and sad faces on animals, cats, and dogs. He is fascinated by people's
facial expressions and draws Figure 3-8, showing faces with fixed
smiles that tell us nothing about an interpersonal aspect; their presence
is mere perceptual identification that he cannot relate beyond a concrete level.

A curious drawing of a bus with loud, silly, and happy faces in its
windows may signal Brian's efforts to experience feelings at 6½ years
(Fig. 3-8). He is working at experiencing feelings and showing
them, though still controlling his response through a clever visual
construct: the bus windows that separate feelings out.

Brian himself acts alternately happy, sad, and angry. He tries on
different faces (Fig. 3-9).

The autistic child and adult have an inborn deficiency in the ability
to abstract, to intuit and, consequently, to understand persons and
situations. Without empathy, the capacity to put oneself in another's
state of mind and to have relationships is blocked. The autistic child

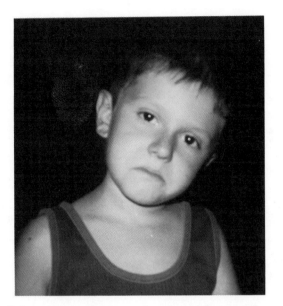

Figure 3-9. Brian puts on a happy, sad, and mad face and draws them. Age, 6 years, 11 months.

and adult acts literally and cannot "read between the lines." Figure 3-10 locates the autistic child in a traditional model of ego functions. In a hypothetical group of autistic personalities, we would likely find severe disturbances in ego functions.[3]

For personal survival the autistic child and adult may also establish "essential geographic territory," a personal space with all the social conventions that denote hierarchy in the outside community. (See Singh, Kay, and Pitman's [1981] discussion of territorial behavior in a phylogenetic approach.) The autistic child and adult may defend physical space to the exclusion of conspecifics, leading to behavior that is stereotyped and rigid. The personality lacks a complex of spatial-temporal behaviors involved in structuring social relations and lacks phenotypic adjustability (the capacity of an organism with a fixed genetic makeup to adapt its behavior flexibly to complicated and changing environmental circumstances).

Walking toward his mother at school, Brian, at age 4 years, passes her by without a glance, as though not wanting to recognize her outside the home.

When asked about school or his teacher, Brian, at age 5½ years,

Figure 3-10. A love-clown looking blankly outward, characteristic of the autistic syndrome wherein interrelationships are blocked through lack of intuition and empathy. Age, 2 years.

curiously says "stop" and refuses attempts to refer to them, as though protecting his territory.

Affect in the Mother-Child Dyad

In a final consideration of autistic personality, Erikson (1963), like other psychoanalysts, regards infancy as a crucial state that strongly influences how our individuality will later develop. He sees the interaction between culture and personality as never-ending, believing that the issues of infancy—trust versus mistrust and autonomy versus shame and doubt—reverberate throughout our life.

Trust versus mistrust may be the key to understanding the mother-autistic child dyad. We may surmise that the autistic child does not establish a basic sense of maternal trust as expected in the first year, and the absence of a reciprocal mother-child bond (influenced by the mother's inappropriate reactions to the child's primitive, abnormal behavior) precludes the normal socializing process and promotes a negative feedback circuit (Goldstein 1959). Although this is an oversimplification of a complex process involving a complicated child, still one cannot help but be impressed with the mothers and fathers who do accomplish bonding interactions with their autistic offspring, proving that such children can develop affiliations (Figs. 3-11 and 3-12). In these special cases, care giving is usually provided by a sensi-

Figure 3-11. Brian's mother's solicitousness, lest he hurt himself, shows maternal bonding behavior. Age, 15 months.

tive, consistent family in which the parents actively impinge on the child in an attempt to promote attachment. Mutual adaptation seems to be key in whether or not parents contribute to the development of an autistic syndrome and become prognostic factors. This is not to imply that parents contribute to the appearance of autism but that they may contribute to its development. Exceptional parents probably miss few

Figure 3-12. A moment of relaxation with father. Accepting ease in a loving and comfortable home. Age, 4 years.

clues given them by their autistic child; their response is therefore adequate, and appropriate in its spontaneity and intensity. They incorporate the autistic child in the family unit in a way that interrupts the autistic process rather than reinforcing it. For discussion of the autistic process, see Clancy and McBride (1969) and Kramer, Anderson, and Westman (1984).

Brian's mother and father accept his peculiarities and force nothing on him, but they do attempt gently to persuade him. He is loved and his home offers easy acceptance.

At age 5½ years, he seeks attention from others, says "Monopoly" to gain the mother's attention, brings books for her, and reads books to her. His affiliation with the mother is evident; he notices her, searches for her when she leaves a room, examines her ear, touches, pulls, and fingers it, and flings himself on her.

He actively seeks attention by negative behavior, plays cat-and-mouse, and at age 5½, waits for a reaction from his father. Father teaches him games that need the cooperation of others—splashing games and hand-catching, where Brian puts his hand on the table and draws it back over and over.

Brian exchanges smiles with a visiting baby and allows it to touch his mouth and eyes and pull his hair. He gives the baby his books to read. Around this time, he attempts to play with other children running around a sprinkler at the park; he runs from splashing water, then splashes too.

He continues to show greater affect in familiar situations and diminished, constricted affect and a strong tendency to withdraw in situations with new people.

In families where the autistic child is carefully treated and where bonding develops, the child can develop cognitive awareness of others, but this may still be at the immature level of object relatedness (Fig. 3-13). That is, when he needs others, he is aware of them; however, when the need has been satisfied, the intrapsychic sense of the other disappears. He can even develop the autonomy that normally forms a major aspect of the lives of 2- and 3-year-old children.

Brian, at age 5½ years, discovers his will and becomes more opinionated, negative, and demanding. He wears certain clothes one day but refuses them another, resulting in an uncoordinated striped and checked outfit.

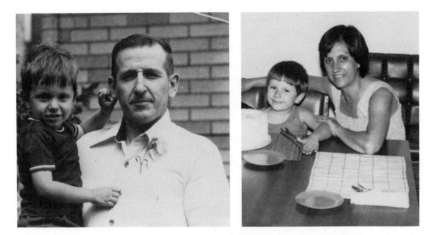

Figure 3-13. Division in interrelations. *Left,* Brian treats his father as an object. Remote and unsmiling, he touches father's ear and button with either hand. *Right,* Brian and his mother are a more complete unit. He shows affect; mother is its source.

Autistic children who are more severely withdrawn may partly recover with psychotherapy. There is no reason why these children, whose disability is due to organic brain disease, should not improve symptomatically through psychotherapy, even though this has no effect on the underlying pathology.

We use incentives in training animals to get the animal to love the trainer. In human beings, love is probably the most important single motivating factor. Autistic children may carry out an activity in response to an order from the trainer but not from anyone else. Routine, consistent activities, performed with love and experience, can give autistic children a sense of security and trust.

From an educational point of view, it is important to treat the autistic child as an individual, not as part of a subgroup. Brian shows more affect and attempts to relate more to his environment and to people when placed, on a trial basis, in a nursery school for normal children. In the hospital program, Brian frequently shows fearful, guarded behavior toward other autistic children who are unpredictable and have more behavioral problems than he. In the nursery school, he attempts to communicate with the children who themselves communicate. This finding replicates Hutt and Hutt's (1970) original observation that on the occasions when truly autistic children make social contacts, their behavior is similar to that of normal children. Brian

Figure 3-14. Brian (second from left) interacting with normal peers. Age, 6
        years, 11 months.

pleases the nursery school teacher and follows the daily routine well.
He is cooperative and attentive. It is important to appreciate the fact
that in the normal nursery school an autistic child is treated as an
individual, not as a member of an autistic group.

The effects on Brian's autism of a period in a nonspecial nursery
school is captured in a photograph of him at age 6 years, 11 months.
Figure 3-14 shows Brian with his classmates and the change is surprising. Brian wants to be part of the group, follows an eight-hour school
day routine, allows physical contact, ventures to interact with others,
and, overall, shows improved affect. (See Kitahara [1983, 1984a,
1984b] for an educational method used in Tokyo, in which autistic
children study and play with their healthy counterparts.)

4

Overall Reflections

Brian continues for about a year to show occasional progress in his expressiveness, until, for no discernible reason, depression shadows the excitement of progress. At age 7, he begins to withdraw: he is in crisis, and his conflict enormous. He sobs "I'm sorry" for angering a teacher in school, as though he blames himself for some disappointment, and often cries out uncontrollably. His figure drawings change into disturbing, robotlike, armless bodies, with blank eyes and firmly shut mouths (Fig. 4-1). Retreat into a hardened facade may be Brian's only defense against terribly lonely feelings. The more his attempts to interact with the environment misfire, the more depressed he becomes.

Brian is transferred from the hospital program to a highly structured private therapeutic day school, where he is in a classroom of about six children who have a variety of learning and behavioral problems. He rides a bus to school each day, fends off more rambunctious children, sits at his own desk, and begins to learn by way of traditional workbooks and curricula. At age 7½, he masters spelling at the 11-year-old level and computes mathematical problems at the 10-year-old level. Although he appears determined in his attempts to read the stories in his reader, he shows poor comprehension of written and spoken words and cannot answer questions about the text.

At the time Brian starts his therapeutic day school, at age 7, his parents are instructed not to provide additional therapy outside school. Accordingly, they turn down offers to place Brian in private therapy with me on a trial basis.

As a result of mutual adjustment—mainly on the part of Brian's

Figure 4-1. At age 7, after a period of progress, Brian became depressed, often crying out uncontrollably, which led to a robotic armless figure. Brian displays his "bad" (torn) sock by drawing a shoe to the side.

parents to his rigid, highly ritualistic habits—the family achieves a certain way of life. Attempts to bring about further change are warded off. Within these limits Brian's personal growth is progressing. He is beginning to identify with his father; there is evidence of a developing self-awareness; in his speech, he is beginning to be consistent in his use of "I." However, he fails to break through to some form of cooperative, productive activity.

The progress Brian makes is a relatively favorable variant among case studies, most of which show poor development, low intelligence, and more aggressive behavior.

For 60 minutes each week Brian receives speech therapy, traditional psychotherapy, and morning group social therapy in his school. He presents himself in a tentative way and is watchful and anxious about people and new situations. The forced intimacy of traditional psycho-therapy, in contrast to nonintrusive therapy that includes bonding procedures, causes him anxiety that in turn leads to rigid, overcontrolled behavior. Because of his low tolerance for physical and verbal contact, it is hard to enter Brian's experiential world. He shows great investment in not revealing feelings, as though his very survival depends on self-protection. He continues to have major difficulty experiencing pleasure relating to others; he takes people for granted and is indifferent toward them.

Brian's mother and father participate in weekly parent therapy sessions at his school and are decreasingly optimistic about his finding ways to relate humanly. After years of talking to Brian, loving him, and faithfully and wholeheartedly supporting every small behavioral gain, they feel tired, stressed, and resigned to Brian's lifelong disorder that appears resistant to known treatment approaches.

Brian's human-figure drawings strengthen the clinical picture. One sees in them his emotional disturbance and his continuing, though diminishing, withdrawal behavior.

Brian produces a drawing (Fig. 4-2) two weeks prior to his 7th year that serves as a summary of his emotional and social adjustment. Two people, together in a boat, stand far apart and face away from each other, not interacting. The drawing communicates an awareness on Brian's part that I may not have noticed otherwise—the beginning sense of relationship to another, which is conspicuously absent in infantile autism as long as intense withdrawal prevails.

Brian's infancy may be deemed the manifestation of the human psyche in vacuo—a human being without relationship to other human beings. Is Brian, as some have contended (Bettelheim 1967; Ekstein and Friedman 1974), a supernatural "messenger of God," a spiritual, celestial being, with superior powers to register subtle, nonverbal expressions and emotions beyond all normal human capabilities—even beyond belief? Is he an "angel" in goodness, innocence, and loveliness, a pure spirit existing on such a high level that he cannot relate to human beings (Fig. 4-3)? On a continuum from illness to superhumanness, Brian seems, in reality, to be an impaired child, his angel-look reflecting his inability to make sense of the environment (Fig. 4-4).

Like an infant, the autistic child neither thinks nor talks, at least on a manifest level. He is aware of things only as they are functional and context-bound. He is indeed a creature living in the world of the "young infant set in the twilight of consciousness" (Anthony 1958).

Figure 4-2. At age 7, Brian continues to make an effort to express feeling in relationships with people.

Figure 4-3. An angel?

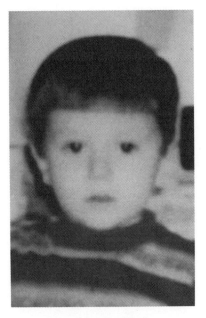

Figure 4-4. Blank.

Brian, at age 7, has not yet attained the capability for enacting a monologue, much less a dialogue; he has attained only the prologue, the language of imagery that is not yet directed to others.

Children and adults may turn to suicide as the only way of protecting themselves from the perpetual fear of catastrophic situations and the terrifying experience of life. However, in patients with brain injuries (Goldstein 1940) and in animals (Berkson 1970; Kling, Lancaster, and Benitone 1970), suicide is an unknown phenomenon, because a decision to commit suicide presupposes that one can account for the situation to oneself and choose death willingly.

Through the case study of Brian, we realize that autism is a more extreme phenomenon than suicide, for the suicidal tendency can be a first step toward becoming active in the world. Infantile autism approaches the extreme negative end of the lifeline; suicide involves a goal-directed action that the autistic child cannot perform. In some ways the autistic child behaves like the lowest form of animal actuated by simple tropisms. He lives an asymbolic life in an uninhabited body with no apparent inner life, not thinking, willing, feeling, or knowing. If there is logic to his behavior, we do not understand it.

5

Case Studies of Two Adolescents

THE CASE OF TING NG

The third largest country in the world geographically, with over 2,000 dialects spoken, China has by far the largest population of any nation—over a billion inhabitants—more than the Soviet Union, India, and Japan combined. Southern Chinese comprise the majority of Chinese in the United States; they tend to be business people, hard working, and consider themselves "good" people.

From this old civilization, with its intense regional rivalries, we find an adolescent case of infantile autism in a Chinese-American male who, at the time of this study, was 16 years of age. The mother is from Hong Kong and speaks Cantonese; the father is from Shanghai and speaks Mandarin Chinese. Because their native dialects differ, they communicate in Mandarin, now taught in Chinese schools as the national language. The parents emigrated to the United States for higher education, met, married while attending school, and now reside in a Chicago community that houses many university professionals. Both mother and father are of high intelligence and work in the field of chemistry.

Ting was born with autism and up until this writing has followed a path very much his own. One of three children, he has an older brother and younger sister, both normal, intelligent, and socially adept. The family members are bilingual and speak Chinese and English fluently, except for Ting, who makes a "good try" at speaking Chinese and is "authentic-sounding." He was severely jaundiced at birth (point 11 on a scale where 1 is considered normal), and at age 3 years was not

Figure 5-1. Tadpolelike human figure drawn through age 6 by autistic Chinese–American male.

developing speech and showed hyperactive behavior. He was diagnosed early as aphasic and autistic by two independent authorities in the field.

As a preschooler, he liked to watch balloons rise in the sky and was generally fascinated by things flying. He liked to paint and watch the paint drip down. His human-figure drawings through his sixth year consistently depict the *Kopffüsser* (Fig. 5-1), a "tadpole figure" (Luquet 1913, 1920), a figure standing on one leg, visibly unstable. Until age 6 years, Ting made incoherent noises and spoke gibberish.

He began to recognize words and used them to speak and read at age 6 years, correlating the written word with the spoken word, eventually giving both meaning. He liked numbers and is still excellent at completing puzzles, but shows a limited attention span, making classroom learning difficult for him. He learns best slowly, in a warm, accepting environment. The slightest harshness can trigger disorganization and upset him; he makes noises to express his frustration. Not until he is 9 years old does Ting's human-figure drawing evolve from tadpolelike figures to a recognizable human figure (Fig. 5-2). Figure 5-2 shows increasing body awareness and the inclusion of essential details such as eyes, ears, nose, mouth, arms, etc.

As a 16-year-old adolescent, Ting looks young for his age, with an immature facies. He enjoys working 500-piece jigsaw puzzles. He attends the Rimland School for autistic children in Evanston, Illinois, named after Bernard Rimland (1964), the well-known researcher in

Figure 5-2. An observing figure with penetrating eyes emerges at 9 years old.

autism. For an adolescent with the autistic syndrome Ting functions optimally.

His growth in affect is reflected in Figure 5-3, which depicts a gentle circus scene, drawn after a visit to the circus. The drawing has rounded, smooth lines and is pleasant to look at. Ting uses color and includes a soft, cuddly dog.

The mother devotes much of her life to his education and supplements his school day with educational and social activity in the home. A college student is hired to spend time with him after school, and

Figure 5-3. Ting, a sweet, gentle boy, shows control of affect in this circus drawing, done at age 14.

eventually a male sitter provides a role model. Ting is carefully treated, receiving the most advanced educational services that the community can provide.

Socially, he develops adaptive appropriate behavior that is not directly comparable to his limited speech, overall borderline intelligence, and rigid compulsive routines. He has a verbal IQ of 68 and a performance IQ of 88; his full-scale IQ is 75 on the Wechsler Adult Intelligence Scale-Revised. His social acceptance of others can be seen in the ease with which he addresses a stranger in his home; he says "Hello," "What is your name?" and shakes hands. He sets the table, serves food to the family, clears the table, and plays on the piano songs taught him by the mother, using both hands and reading the music. He occupies himself listening to records and uses the stereo spontaneously. With prompting, he keeps a diary and writes a short paragraph after each dinner describing the meal and the family members. He follows commands and generally (about 90% of the time) answers questions accurately. His speech is robotic, clipped and telegraphic, and he must be coaxed to express his thoughts in fuller sentences. A sample conversation would be:

Question: Do you want more food, Ting?
Ting: A little more.

Question: Where are we going tomorrow?
Ting: Water Tower, Kroch and Brentano's book, Marshall Field's.

Question: Shouldn't we wait and go next week?
Ting: No, go tomorrow, Kroch and Brentano's book.

Question: What did you do in school today?
Ting: Movie.

Question: What was the movie about?
Ting: Horse is like Black Beauty.

When the task is not of his choosing, Ting draws perfunctorily and without affective expression. Asked to draw a human figure, he draws first a female, then, with the mother's coaching he produces a male (Fig. 5-4).

Toward his mother, Ting displays affiliation and attachment, using a "help" call (or "bond" signal in Tinbergen and Tinbergen's [1972] sense) to gain her attention. Mother typically responds, "Yes, do you want to tell me something?"

Figure 5-4. Human-figure drawing by a 16-year-old autistic Chinese–American male. Both figures show inanimate appearance and premature aging.

When mother leaves to go to a meeting, Ting gives her puzzles to take with her (a bonding behavior), possibly a way of reminding her to come back. At bedtime, he comes downstairs after putting on his pajamas, says, "Good night, mommy," kisses her, and shakes my hand. We find him sitting at the top of the stairs waiting for mother to tuck him in.

At 16 years old, Ting has strong gaze aversion and little facial expression. His perpetually flat, nonexpressive face is in part due to his Oriental heritage in which facial musculature is less developed and variable than that of Caucasians. When frustrated, his manner is that of a 3- or 4-year-old child, overactive and jumping from one activity to the next.

In contrast, he also shows the autistic savant capacity for complex calendrical calculations. He is able instantly to correlate the Western calendar with the Chinese lunar calendar, with its 12 zodiac years and sacred animals. Although Ting has unique memory abilities, he is

Figure 5-5. Artistic mastery develops in adolescence, here showing cartoon
figures. Age, 16 years.

unable to use money independently or go to the store because he walks
away after purchasing an item, leaving the change behind. In one
instance, the father discovers while shopping that his son has exactly
$10.97 in his wallet (Ting does not think of the tax) for a set of plastic
models that he spotted on their last visit to the store, two months prior!
Later, it is discovered that exactly $10.97 is missing from the mother's
wallet. Father asks, ''Where did you get this money?'' Ting responds,
''Mommy's purse.'' He makes excited noises when the father refuses
to engage in mathematical games with him following the incident.
Mother says, ''Stop noise,'' and he does.

Ting has no sense of success, pride, satisfaction, or purpose. He is
at his best in routine, highly structured situations, preferring to stick at
a certain level, and must be forced, gradually and gently, into new
experiences and learning. Having gotten hold of the book *Transac-
tional Analysis for Tots* (Freed 1973), he shows definite interest, reading it over and over. Given a page number, he can recite the entire
page verbatim. For instance, after losing the father's umbrella and
gloves in a department store, Ting recites from the book, ''angry,
anxiety, worry, concern.'' He then states, ''People can disagree and be
angry with each other and still love each other.'' Over the next two
years he quotes from the book, appropriately matching text to situation.

Ting develops a delusional autistic mode of adjustment during his
16th year and is happiest when he can withdraw. When interrupted, he
invariably spills out superhero verbiage. Superheroes are a consuming

Figure 5-6. This drawing of a parade is for a greeting card. Note the center drummer's detached arm. Age, 16 years.

interest, "the weirder, the better," says the mother. He collects superhero comic books in a huge stack in his bedroom and knows their exact order—if one is missing, he will not settle down until he finds it. He constantly draws and colors superheroes (Fig. 5-5) and looks forward to trips to the newsstand to purchase superhero comics. He even assigns superhero names to people at camp, calling one female Dyna Girl. Although at camp he never relates directly to her, when he returns home he fantasizes about Dyna Girl in imagined superhero scenarios. Through superhero dramas Ting enlivens his emotions and projects affect.

Figure 5-5 demonstrates Ting's remarkably accurate and meticulous ability to draw images from memory. Ting began drawing—an activity engaged in by only a few high-functioning autistic children—in childhood. In adolescence, he gains competency using various mediums, though always applied with a controlled, miniscule stroke, preferably with a toothpick. Ting draws a Christmas card for me (on file) and addresses the envelope himself. The card, a picture of "The Nutcracker," a ballet he enjoyed seeing that week, shows a very carefully detailed scene, with a stoic-faced toy soldier in the center.

Ting likes parades and creates a card (Fig. 5-6) showing musicians marching confidently and gaily. Music catches his fancy and he uses

Figure 5-7. An adolescent case of infantile autism. Ting, age 16 years, walks with his sister while at summer camp. Hunched shoulders, tucked-in head, and arm placed awkwardly off his sister's shoulder show lack of normal response to an affectionate caress.

abstract symbols to suggest music on the card. Ting's body language is rigid and, although his drawing shows some movement, the marchers, in profile, avert their eyes from the viewer. Affect is conspicuous, controlled, and smoothly expressed: he writes, "Happy Thanksgiving to Mom and Dad and Chi. Love Ting." (See O'Gorman [1970]; and Tanguay [1984] for a classification of types of defenses, including monotonous graphic production, used by autistic children to cope with reality.)

Ting continues until age 19 to attend the Rimland School, along with three Afro-Americans, and 16 European-Americans. He is in a classroom of four young adults with one teacher and one teacher's aide. Vocational training is emphasized, but a recent attempt to hold a job in a residence hall of a university leads to minimal success. Given the task of shelving cereal boxes, he prefers examining the cartoon character illustrations on the boxes. Apprehensive in a strange environment, he begins grinding his teeth. In times of tension and excitement he goes down on all fours, rocking and whining. He occasionally sniffs, flicks, waves his hands, and postures with his trunk. Overall, during adolescence, his condition remains stable (Fig. 5-7).

HUMAN-FIGURE DRAWING IN THE PSYCHODIAGNOSIS
OF AN AUTISTIC ADOLESCENT

By adolescence, the outcome of infantile autism can be seen to vary, depending on the organic damage, maturational patterns, and family structure. The following case study looks briefly at the effects of autism in an adolescent named Kenneth.[1] He differs from Ting in having higher language and social skills, and more aggressive behavior.

I first examined Kenneth, a male of Lithuanian background residing in a middle-class suburb of Chicago, when he was 12 years old. His father is an electrician, a cordial and firm man, quite dedicated to his family. His mother is a housewife—a warm, friendly woman who is pleasant and caring.

Kenneth was brought for psychological examination because of his communication disorder and alternately withdrawn and aggressive behavior. During severe outbursts he would throw furniture and bite bystanders. He is hyperactive, expressionless, and makes no eye contact. He tries to get away from people, and shows no affection. Kenneth was born five weeks prematurely "two weeks after my water bag broke," says the mother; she feels this has some bearing on his problem. He had not developed speech by the age of 4 years. An electroencephalogram is normal; a computerized brain tomogram shows a mild dilation of the left lateral ventricle suggesting slight underdevelopment of the left cerebral hemisphere, a finding fairly frequently reported in autistic children (Campbell et al. 1982). Recent psychological testing indicates overall borderline intelligence (IQ of 70 on the Wechsler Intelligence Scale for Children-Revised), with a marked discrepancy between verbal and performance scores in favor of the latter—an expected finding. No focal neurological signs appear on the annual neurological examination, performed by Peter Huttenlocher, pediatric neurologist at the University of Chicago.

Kenneth's physical appearance at age 12 years shows motor deficit, tibial torsion of the right foot, and some speech imperfection. He is impulsive, mildly hyperactive, has a short attention span, and catastrophic reactions with a "sudden run" when overwhelmed by his surroundings. He tends to smile with the right side of his face but not with the left, an observation reported by the mother. His affect is flat and mechanical, as is his speech, and he shows strong gaze aversion during social contact by burying his head in a TV guide or football schedule that he carries around with him. He initially does not respond to me and withdraws from any attempts at interpersonal interaction. He occasionally flaps his hands, rocks, laughs to himself, drools, stutters, and hits his own leg.

By age 12 his understanding of verbal commands has improved and he engages in simple conversation. He appears to be an affectionate and sensitive child and quite unexpectedly kisses me good-bye on a clinic visit.

At the University of Chicago and one other major medical center he was diagnosed (with follow-up reevaluation every two years) as meeting the criteria for infantile autism set forth by DSM-III-Revised (American Psychiatric Association 1987):

- Qualitative impairment in reciprocal social interaction
- Qualitative impairment in verbal and nonverbal communication and in imaginary activity
- Markedly restricted repertoire of activities and interests
- Onset of disorder during infancy or childhood

In the initial diagnostic interview, Kenneth is asked to complete a human-figure drawing (Fig. 5-8). He continues to make human-figure drawings (Figs. 5-8 through 5-15) between the ages of 12 and 16.

The first drawing (Fig. 5-8), with its bared teeth and stick fingers, generates a number of working hypotheses. Such teeth reflect oral aggression (Machover 1949; Levy 1958) and autistic symptoms involving rage such as occur in a number of autistic children on reaching adolescence. His primitive aggression and assaultiveness are further indicated by the stick fingers with no hands (Machover 1949; Hammer 1958).

Kenneth's defective life is suggested by a disproportionately large head with limbs and no trunk, reflecting overvaluation of the brain due to the frustration of being mentally retarded (Machover 1951). The figure's feet do not touch the ground, and being high up on the page, the drawing looks adrift, demonstrating insecurity (Machover 1949) and fantasy rather than reality satisfaction (Buck 1958).

A very different self is represented in the next drawing (Fig. 5-9), made six months later. Two characteristics dominate the drawing—again the bared teeth reflecting oral aggression (Machover 1949; Levy 1958), and fingers with no hands that portray infantile aggression and assaultiveness (Machover 1949). Lack of a neck demonstrates a lack of impulse control; the tight-belted waistline—the line of demarcation

Figure 5-8–Figure 5-11. Fig. 5-8 (upper left): Kenneth, age 12 years. The beginning of oral aggression during adolescence can be seen in a first drawing.   Fig. 5-9 (upper right): Kenneth, age 12½ years. Efforts to constrain poorly controlled affect (shown in the failure to draw a neck) are suggested in the belted waistline. Fingers and a lack of hands suggest assaultiveness. Fig. 5-10 (lower left): Perseveration of identical figures that are noninteracting and poorly differentiated demonstrate repetitive behavior continuing into adolescence.   Fig. 5-11 (lower right): Kenneth, age 13 years. Psychotic features are evident in Kenneth's robotic figure—a result of his losing affect control to a psychologically disorganizing degree.

between the chest area of physical power and the genital region—
reveals Kenneth's efforts to control affect (Machover 1951). The
buckle indicates dependency (see Wing [1983] on autistic adolescents'
social and interpersonal needs); the asymmetry of the legs implies poor
coordination (Machover 1949).

The second and third drawings are made on the same day. Figure
5-10 depicts Kenneth's monotonous graphic production, typical of
autistic children and here continuing into adolescence.

During this time Kenneth is in nonintrusive therapy with me once
every three weeks, and his projective drawings are used as guides. He is
in a residential program at the Lt. Joseph P. Kennedy, Jr., School for
Exceptional Children, Chicago, returning home on weekends. During
summer vacation he attends speech camp where he receives intensive
speech therapy. His parents are very involved with the residential
program. They both feel considerable anguish over Kenneth's non-
compliant behavior, but slowly become better able to deal with him.
Kenneth adjusts fairly well to the residential program; the mother has
difficulty separating from him. Kenneth still is impulsive, has a short
attention span, and low tolerance for frustration. His behavior becomes
more self-abusive and self-stimulating, and his tantrums increase,
creating management problems for the school staff.

To aid in evaluating Kenneth's condition at this time, the human-
figure drawing (Fig. 5-11) is readministered. The succession of drawings (Figs. 5-9, 5-10, and 5-11) adds data that strengthen the clinical
picture. Figure 5-11, drawn approximately six months after the second
and third drawings, shows irregularities so pronounced as to indicate
psychotic disorganization (Machover 1951). Gross disproportion,
body distortions, and his failure to recognize the grotesqueness of the
drawing demonstrate psychosis (Machover 1949; Levy 1958); omis-
sion of arms further indicates an emotional crisis, withdrawal, and
depression (Machover 1949, 1951) that can presage bizarre behavior
and eventual breakdown (Wing 1981; Wolff and Chick 1980).

Kenneth incurs disciplinary action at the school, and has to be
physically restrained for the first time. He repeatedly cries, ''I'm
sorry,'' into the next day, and talks gibberish day and night, even in
his sleep, for two weeks afterward. His drawing (Fig. 5-11) has
''blocks over his body.'' It is a male robot figure that reveals Kenneth's feeling of being controlled by outside forces (Hammer 1958).
The clownlike mouth shows inappropriate affect or forced amiability

Figure 5-12–Figure 5-15. Fig. 5-12 (upper left): Kenneth, age 13½ years. Pop-eyes with long lashes show sexual excitement in adolescence.   Fig. 5-13 (upper right): Kenneth, age 14 years. A grotesque, masked figure with spear-like fingers shows Kenneth's overwhelming affect and illustrates his prevailing withdrawal mixed with aggressive outbursts.   Fig. 5-14 (lower left): Kenneth, age 15 years. A dramatic change in protective defenses results in a small, inhibited figure with mittened hands as Kenneth shows intense effort to control affect.   Fig. 5-15 (lower right): Kenneth, age 16 years. An immature and socially acceptable figure develops with age and psychotherapy. Forced amiability is suggested in the fixed smile.

(Machover 1949). Rigid posture demonstrates defensiveness (Hammer 1958) and rigid emotional controls (Levy 1958).

Figure 5-12, drawn approximately six months later, further demonstrates the progression of therapy. Between the fourth and fifth drawings (Figs. 5-11 and 5-12), Kenneth receives pharmacotherapy (Mellaril) and individual nonintrusive therapy for 45 minutes every three weeks.

Kenneth continues to have severe social-affective problems that manifest in his withdrawal, rigid-obsessional behavior, gaze aversion, fear, and language difficulties. He shows excessive masturbatory behavior. Figure 5-12 is "pop-eyed," showing sexual excitation, the long lashes emphasizing exhibitionism and sexual appeal (Machover 1951). Oral aggression and assaultiveness are again reflected in teeth baring (Machover 1949; Levy 1958) and in the fingers without hands (Machover 1949). His effort to keep control is again conveyed by the belted waistline (Machover 1949).

Figure 5-13 is completed six months later. Kenneth improves in maintaining eye contact, but his affect remains flat. He stutters, masturbates, and is impulsive and extremely excitable, often flapping his hands. In this drawing, the human figure is grotesquely distorted, with massive body and limbs. It occupies the entire length of the page and is shifted to the left. Its spear fingers without hands indicate an aggressive psychopath with feelings of inadequacy, again showing assaultiveness as described by Machover (1949). A concave mouth demonstrates intemperate outbursts (Machover 1951), the closed, masked eyes reflect caution and secretiveness (Hammer 1958), and exclusion of the environment (Machover 1951).

In the therapy sessions, his interpersonal interaction gradually improves from between 50% to 100%, but outside the family he still remains reserved and socially isolated. (See Rutter [1970] on report of improvement in social and interpersonal skills during adolescence in autism.) He draws figure 5-14 a year later, at age 15, a stick figure that reflects insecurity (Levy 1958) or evasion and negativism (Hammer 1958). This figure too has a clownlike mouth suggesting forced amiability (Machover 1949).

In Figure 5-14, the pupil, the seeing portion of the eye, is omitted, reflecting his egocentric character, which feeds parasitically on what he views; the eye is not used as an instrument of objective discrimination (Machover 1951). Kenneth's problem in the expression and control of affect is seen in the mittened hands, again suggesting repressed aggression, and with the lack of feet, discouragement (Machover 1949). The entire drawing being shifted to the left side of the page indicates tension (Machover 1949) and reflects a need for structure (Hammer 1958).

The eighth drawing (Fig. 5-15), one year later, depicts inhibition (Machover 1949). An awareness of physical impulses (Buck 1958; Machover 1951) is expressed in the elongated neck with handless stick fingers, indicating an assaultive subject; an effort to control affect is again evidenced by the belted waistline (Machover 1951).

At the age of 16 years, Kenneth shows less discrepancy between his social-affective and intellectual behavior (Rutter and Schopler 1978) with borderline intelligence (Wechsler Intelligence Scale for Children-Revised) and "pseudo-social" (Goldstein 1959) behavior (Schopler and Mesibov 1983). His verbal IQ is 62 and performance IQ is 90 on the Wechsler Scale and suggests no significant change in intellectual function. Socially he is developing adaptive and appropriate behavior that is not directly comparable to the degree of organic pathology. This hypothesis is further supported by the relatively normal but immature appearance seen in Figure 5-15. Kenneth reveals an egocentric character that does not observe the environment (demonstrated by the empty eye with no pupil); pseudo-social behavior and forced amiability are suggested by the clownlike smile (Machover 1949). While Kenneth's outward appearance is normal, his human-figure drawing lacks human spirit and feeling. The therapy is continued.[1]

FOLLOW-UP STUDIES

Some common ground is emerging in the literature on follow-up studies of children diagnosed as having early infantile autism. (See DeMyer, Hingtgen, and Jackson's [1981] review of a decade of research in infantile autism.) We find that 50% to 70% of children diagnosed with infantile autism have poor outcomes; 30% to 50% are institutionalized. Approximately 20% develop seizures during adolescence, which occur more frequently in those who have an IQ of 50 or less; 75% test within the mentally retarded range, while 60% of all autistic children have IQs below 50. Infrequently, there is a report of an autistic adult being married, having children, and living a successful life. For example, a professor, who is a wealthy international researcher in psychiatry, has a son with autism and claims this outcome. Odd reports will always be found that cannot be confirmed and may reflect a variation of the disease.

The literature concurs that no one treatment is useful with all autistic children. Autism is not a homogeneous disorder; infectious, metabolic, genetic, and traumatic factors have all been convincingly implicated in the genesis of the autistic syndrome, reflecting diverse causative insults to the central nervous system. Generally, autistic individuals do not achieve a self-supportive adulthood or completely normal social adjustment. Many develop rituals and become aggressive. If there is language before 5 years of age, the prognosis is better. Autism appears to occur in families with chronically ill children.

Many autistic children have savant ability and can perform special feats. Almost all have strengths. In a hypothetical group, we would likely find that several read, write, and have communication skills; however, compared to their peers, their ability in these areas is far below normal.

Autism does not follow social class cross-culturally; the syndrome occurs in other countries. Ritvo has found autism in Africa, France, and India (Ritvo and Freeman 1978), and B. L. Leventhal (per. com. February 1983) reported a case of infantile autism at the University of Chicago in a 7-year-old bilingual Polish boy.

A range of autistic behavioral manifestations are predetermined. The majority of autistic children improve as they mature, but maturation patterns vary enormously, as do outcomes. Many autistic individuals, in whom adaptive appropriate behavior is not directly comparable with the degree of organic pathology, can be taught specific skills and behaviors.

6

Summary

This study has tried to provide an appreciation of the way in which hereditary and environmental factors interactively contribute to autism. A holistic study of autism starts with the premise that both genetic defect and environmental triggering mechanisms play significant roles.

Autism was examined in a male, aged 3 to 7 years, of South American-middle European parents, based on the hypothesis that (a) a combined etiology comprised of biological (genetic variations) and environmental (stress) factors induces autistic aberration during the entire course of affect development, and (b) biology and culture are neither opposed to nor separate from whatever initiates autistic behavior.

The approach to this study was derived from Goldstein's (1939) theory of the organism as a whole, which regards behavior in its full biological context and emphasizes biological factors, for only within a holistic framework is autism understandable.

The study investigated the problem of affect mobilization and control. Withdrawal and affectlessness in autism were discussed as a protective mechanism having survival and adaptive significance, and as the sign of a primary organic lesion in the central nervous system involving deficiencies in the representational function. Also investigated were relationships between affect and cognition as affect development parallels Piaget's ([1947] 1950, [1926] 1951a, [1929] 1951b, [1936] 1952, [1937] 1954, [1926] 1955, [1952] 1957, [1945] 1962, [1946] 1969) and Piaget and Inhelder's ([1948] 1956, [1966] 1969) study of intellectual development. Arrested development at the sensorimotor-preconcept level of intelligence was demonstrated and found

to significantly influence affect as well as interpersonal relations, and
to exacerbate the autistic child's asocial deviation. The concept of
affective–cognitive symbiosis was explored and cognition was found
to control affect and the ability to cope with environmental stimulation.

Case material, obtained from direct observations and from mini-
studies, was analyzed in a framework of motor, intelligence, language,
and affect development. Inquiry into two adolescent cases of autism
(one of Chinese origin representing a cross-cultural case of autism)
was made to establish a basis for predicting probable future development of phylogenetically derived capacities.

The identification by Piaget and Inhelder ([1966] 1969) of graphic
images (drawing) as diagnostic for the development of intelligence and
for evaluating the representation process has value insofar as human-
figure drawings serve to explicate autism. Drawing has long been used
as a readily accessible means of eliciting nonverbal communication
from children and for psychodiagnosis. Successive human-figure
drawings were presented and interpreted and found to reflect the psychological activity in a young child and two adolescents and to be
useful for assessing affect, social perception, and cognitive abilities.
How far such drawing skill advances other communication skills is
unknown.

Some may question whether human-figure drawings of autistic children have diagnostic value. In a personal communication (24 September 1983), B. Bettelheim stated that, based on his 29 years' experience, drawings of autistic children do not have high discriminative
value in the sense that one cannot tell whether a child is autistic by
drawings alone. Generally, Bettelheim considers the value of drawings
dependent on the level of expertise in interpreting them.

In this same communication, Bettelheim stated that he knows of no
available documented work on the human-figure drawing of autistic
children. Indeed, a computerized literature search has failed to reveal
any such publication.[1] Random drawing by autistic children is easier to
obtain than specific drawing. In addition, it is extremely difficult to
obtain human-figure drawings by autistic children because they tend
not to draw human figures.

Taken at face value, some may argue that *Nadia: A Case of Extraordinary Drawing Ability in an Autistic Child* (Selfe 1977) is a well-
documented case. However, the case of Nadia is not a psychological
study, and no history or analysis is provided. Moreover, it is a book of

horse figures, not human figures. Nadia lost her talent for drawing as her language skills improved, according to Selfe's report, which brings into question the validity of the diagnosis. Indeed, Nadia tried hard to please others with her drawings and understood that people liked them, thereby showing more insight into others than is usual among the autistic. Autistic children as well as normal children generally do not lose a talent; they improve it. Some may argue that Bettelheim (1967) himself used human-figure drawings in his work with the autistic; however, the drawings appear to have been an afterthought, for he drew no conclusions from them. Further, the literature has not been statistically clean prior to the new diagnostic criteria for classifying autism (American Psychiatric Association 1987). Misdiagnosis has led to errors in sample selection and misinterpretation of important research as late as 1978, the year in which the leading journal in this area changed its name from *Journal of Autism and Childhood Schizophrenia* to *Journal of Autism and Developmental Disorders*. Thus, this study provides human-figure drawing by autistic children that exists nowhere else in the literature and, by means of these three studies, suggests the psychodiagnostic significance of such drawing.

These data could eventually permit an even broader analysis and be followed by studies comparing the human-figure drawing of autistic children with those of other diagnostic groups such as mental retardates. There is much promise for research in this area.

Investigative groups are currently running independently of each other. A major goal of my studies (Seifert 1990a, 1990b) was to bring together in one place results of minor and major studies of behavior within the context of a biological explanation of autism. Two opposing theoretical systems were compared—psychoanalytic theory and modern evolutionary theory—and the latter, as expressed in Freedman's (Freedman, Loring, and Martin 1967) biological approach to personality, was confirmed.

By appreciating the part played by heredity and the environment in autism, these studies provide an understanding of autism not heretofore described.

Notes

1. INFANTILE AUTISM

1. Seifert, C. D. 1988a. Learning from drawings: an autistic child looks out at us. *The American Journal of Art Therapy*, 27(2), pp. 45–53. (Used by permission of the publisher.)

3. AFFECT AND AUTISM

1. "Turning toward" is defined by the behavioristic term *Zuwendung*.
2. There are many varied definitions of motivation, as shown by Cofer and Appley (1964). One that fits my interests is that of Young (1961), who refers to motivation as the process of arousing action, sustaining the activity in progress, and regulating the pattern of activity.
3. Model of ego functions and their components: reality testing, judgment, sense of reality, regulation and control of drives, affects, and impulses; object relations, thought processes, adaptive regression in the service of the ego; and defensive functioning, stimulus barrier, autonomous functioning, synthetic-integrative functioning, and mastery competence (Bellak 1977).

5. CASE STUDIES OF TWO ADOLESCENTS

1. Seifert, C. D. 1988b. The human-figure drawing in the treatment of an autistic adolescent. *Child Psychiatry and Human Development*, 19(1), pp. 74–81. (Used by permission of the publisher.)

6. SUMMARY

1. Ninety-two data bases were included: Psychological Abstracts, Dissertation Abstracts International, Educational Research Information Center, and Medline from October 1983 through 1967; Science Citation Index from 1980 through 1978; and a manual search of *Buros Mental Measurements Yearbook* (Buros), September 1983 through 1949.

References

American Psychiatric Association. 1987. *Diagnostic and Statistical Manual of Mental Disorders.* 3rd ed. Rev. Washington: American Psychiatric Association.

Anthony, J. 1958. An experimental approach to the psychopathology of childhood: autism. *British Journal of Medical Psychology* 31:211–25.

Bauman, M., and Kemper, T. L. 1985. Histoanatomic observations of the brain in early infantile autism. *Neurology* 35:866–74.

Beery, K. E. 1967a. *Developmental Test of Visual-Motor Integration.* Chicago: Follett.

———. 1967b. *Developmental Test of Visual-Motor Integration. Administration and Scoring Manual.* Chicago: Follett.

Bell, C. C. 1980. States of consciousness. *Journal of the National Medical Association* 72:331–34.

———. 1982. Black intrapsychic survival skills: alteration of states of consciousness. *Journal of the National Medical Association* 74:1017–20.

Bellak, L. 1977. Psychiatric states in adults with minimal brain dysfunction. *Psychiatric Annals* 7:58–75.

Bender, L. 1938. *A Visual Motor Gestalt Test and Its Clinical Use.* American Orthopsychiatric Association Research Monograph 3.

———. 1946. *Bender Motor Gestalt Test: Cards and Manual Instructions.* New York: American Orthopsychiatric Association, Inc.

Benjamin, J. D. 1963. Further comments on some developmental aspects of anxiety. In *Counterpoint,* edited by H. Gaskill, pp. 121–53. New York: International Universities Press.

Benson, D. F. 1979. *Aphasia, Alexia, and Agraphia.* New York: Churchill Livingstone.

Bergman, P., and Escalona, S. 1949. Unusual sensitivities in very young children. *Psychoanalytic Study of the Child* 3–4:334–52.

Berkson, G. 1970. Defective infants in a feral monkey group. *Folia Primatologica* 12:284–89.

Bettelheim, B. 1967. *The Empty Fortress: Infantile Autism and the Birth of the Self.* New York: Free Press.

Bettelheim, Bruno. 24 September 1983. Telephone conversation with author.

Blomquist, H. K., Bohman, M., Edvinsson, S. O., Gillberg, C., Gustavson, K. H., Holmgren, G., and Wahlström, J. 1985. Frequency of the fragile X syndrome in infantile autism. A Swedish multicenter study. *Clinical Genetics* 27(2):113–17.

Brask, B. H. 1970. ''A Prevalence Investigation of Childhood Psychosis.''

Paper presented at the meeting of the Scandinavian Congress of Psychiatry.

Brown, W. T., Jenkins, E. C., Friedman, E., Brooks, J., Wisniewski, K., Raguthu, S., and French, J. 1982. Autism is associated with the fragile X syndrome. *Journal of Autism and Developmental Disorders* 12:303–308.

Buck, N. 1958. The case of R: before and after therapy. In *The Clinical Application of Projective Drawings,* edited by E. F. Hammer, pp. 276–308. Springfield, Ill.: Thomas.

Bühler, C., and Hetzer, H. 1928. Das erste Verständnis für Ausdruck im ersten Lebensjahr [The first understanding of expression in the first year of life]. *Zeitschrift für Psychologie und Physiologie der Sinnesorgane* 107:50–61.

Buros, O. K., ed., 1949–83. *Buros Mental Measurements Yearbook.* Highland Park, N.J.: Gryphon Press.

Campbell, M., Rosenbloom, S., Perry, R., George, A. E., Kricheff, I. I., Anderson, L., Small, A. M., and Jennings, S. 1982. Computerized tomographic (CT) scans involving young autistic children. *American Journal of Psychiatry* 139:510–12.

Cattell, P. 1940. *The Measurement of Intelligence of Infants and Young Children.* Reprint 1960. New York: Johnson Reprint Corporation.

Clancy, H., and McBride, G. 1969. The autistic process and its treatment. *Journal of Child Psychology and Psychiatry, and Applied Disciplines* 10:233–44.

Cofer, C. N., and Appley, M. H. 1964. *Motivation: Theory and Research.* New York: Wiley.

Courchesne, E., Yeung-Courchesne, R., Press, G. A., Hesselink, J. R., and Jernigan, T. L. 1988. Hypoplasia of cerebellar vernal lobules VI and VII in autism. *New England Journal of Medicine* 318(21):1349–54.

DeMyer, M. K., Hingtgen, J. N., and Jackson, R. K. 1981. Infantile autism reviewed: a decade of research. *Schizophrenia Bulletin* 7:388–451.

Ekman, P., and Friesen, W. 1975. *Unmasking the Face.* Englewood Cliffs, N.J.: Prentice-Hall.

Ekstein, R., and Friedman, S. W. 1974. Infantile autism: from entity to process. *Reiss-Davis Clinic Bulletin* 11:70–85.

Engel, G. L., and Schmale, A. H. 1972. Conservation withdrawal: a primary regulatory process of organismic homeostasis. In *Physiology, Emotion, and Psychosomatic Illness: CIBA Foundation, Symposium No. 8,* edited by Board of Editors, pp. 57–85. Amsterdam: Associated Scientific Publishers.

Erikson, E. H. 1963. *Childhood and Society.* 2nd ed. New York: Norton.

Fein, D., Braverman, M., Pennington, B., Markowitz, P., and Waterhouse, L. 1986. Toward a neuropsychological model of infantile autism: are the social deficits primary? *Journal of the American Academy of Child Psychiatry* 25(2):198–212.

Freed, A. M. 1973. *TA for Tots.* Sacramento, Calif.: Jalmar Press.

Freedman, D. G. 1961. The infant's fear of strangers and the flight response. *Journal of Child Psychology and Psychiatry* 4:242–48.

———. 1974. *Human Infancy: An Evolutionary Perspective.* New York: Wiley.

Freedman, Daniel G. 30 July 1984. Interview with author. Chicago, Illinois.

Freedman, D. G., Loring, C. B., and Martin, R. M. 1967. Emotional behavior and personality development. In *Infancy and Early Childhood: A Handbook and Guide to Human Development,* edited by Y. Brackbill, pp. 429–502. New York: Free Press.

Freud, S. [1900] 1953. The interpretation of dreams. In *Standard Edition of the Complete Psychological Works of Sigmund Freud.* Translated by J. Strachey, vols. 4 and 5. London: Hogarth Press. (Original work published in 1900 as *Die Traumdeutung.*)

———.[1920] 1955*a*. Beyond the pleasure principle. In *Standard Edition of the Complete Psychological Works of Sigmund Freud.* Translated by J. Strachey, vol. 18, pp. 7–64. London: Hogarth Press. (Original work published in 1920 as *Jenseits des Lustprinzips.*)

———.[1913] 1955*b*. Totem and taboo and other works. In *Standard Edition of the Complete Psychological Works of Sigmund Freud.* Translated by J. Strachey, vol. 13, pp. ix–162. London: Hogarth Press. (Original work published in 1913 as *Totem und Tabu.*)

———.[1936] 1959. Inhibition, symptoms and anxiety. In *Standard Edition of the Complete Psychological Works of Sigmund Freud.* Translated by J. Strachey, vol. 20, pp. 87–172. London: Hogarth Press. (Original work published in 1936 as *Hemmung, Symptom und Angst.*)

Gallup, G. G., Jr., and Maser, J. D. 1977. Tonic immobility: evolutionary underpinnings of human catalepsy and catatonia. In *Psychopathology: Experimental Models,* edited by J. D. Maser and M. E. P. Seligman, pp. 334–57. San Francisco: Freeman.

Geschwind, N., Quadfasel, F. A., and Segarra, J. 1968. Isolation of the speech area. *Neuropsychologia* 6:327–40.

Gesell, A., and Ilg, F. L. 1943. *Infant and Child in the Culture of Today: The Guidance of Development in Home and Nursery School.* New York: Harper.

Goldfarb, W. 1964. An investigation of childhood schizophrenia. *Archives of General Psychiatry* 11(2):620–34.

Goldstein, K. 1939. *The Organism.* New York: American Books.

———. 1940. *Human Nature in the Light of Psychopathology.* Cambridge, Mass.: Harvard University Press.

———. 1959. Abnormal conditions in infancy. *Journal of Nervous and Mental Disease* 128:538–57.

Goldstein, K., and Scheerer, M. 1941. Abstract and concrete behavior: an experimental study with special tests. *Psychological Monographs* 53:1–151.

Gray, W. S., and Robinson, H. M. 1963. *Gray Oral Reading Test.* Indianapolis: Bobbs-Merrill.

Haber, R. N., and Haber, R. B. 1964. Eidetic imagery: I. frequency. *Perceptual and Motor Skills* 19:131–38.

Hammer, E. 1958. *The Clinical Application of Projective Drawings.* Springfield, Ill.: Thomas.

Hebb, D. O., and Riesen, A. H. 1943. The genesis of emotional fears. *Bulletin of the Canadian Psychological Association* 3:49–50.

Hoshino, Y., Manome, T., Kaneko, M., Yashima, Y., and Kumashiro, H. 1984. Computed tomography of the brain in children with early infantile autism. *Folia Psychiatrica et Neurologica Japonica* 38(1):33–43.

Hutt, S. J., and Hutt, C. 1970. *Direct Observation and Measurement of Behaviour.* Springfield, Ill.: Thomas.

Huttenlocher, P. R., and Huttenlocher, J. 1973. A study of children with hyperlexia. *Neurology* 23:1107–16.

Jersild, A. T. 1954. Emotional development. In *Manual of Child Psychology,* 2nd ed., edited by L. Carmichael, pp. 833–917. New York: Wiley.

Kanner, L. 1943. Autistic disturbances of affective contact. *Nervous Child* 2:217–50.

―――. 1971. Follow-up study of 11 autistic children originally reported in 1943. *Journal of Autism and Childhood Schizophrenia* 1:119–145.

King, P. D. 1975. Early infantile autism: relation to schizophrenia. *Journal of the American Academy of Child Psychiatry* 14:666–82.

Kitahara, K. 1983. *Daily Life Therapy.* Vol. 1, *Principles and Methods.* Boston: Nimrod.

―――. 1984a. *Daily Life Therapy.* Vol. 2, *Record of Actual Education at Musashino Higashi Gakuen School.* Boston: Nimrod.

―――. 1984b. *Daily Life Therapy.* Vol. 3, *Physical Education.* Boston: Nimrod.

Kling, A., Lancaster, J., and Benitone, J. 1970. Amygdalectomy in the free-ranging vervet (*Cercopithecus aethiops*). *Journal of Psychiatric Research* 7:191–99.

Klüver, H. 1965. Neurobiology of normal and abnormal perception. In *Psychopathology of Perception,* edited by P. Hoch and J. Zubin, pp. 1–40. New York: Grune & Stratton.

Korner, A. F. 1971. Individual differences at birth: implications for early experience and later development. *American Journal of Orthopsychiatry* 41:608–19.

Kramer, D. A., Anderson, R. B., and Westman, J. C. 1984. The corrective autistic experience: an application of the models of Tinbergen and Mahler. *Child Psychiatry and Human Development* 15:104–20.

Kubicek, L. F. 1980. Organization in two mother–infant interactions involving a normal infant and his fraternal twin brother who was later diagnosed as autistic. In *High Risk Infants and Children,* edited by S. Goldberg, pp. 99–100. New York: Academic Press.

Largo, R. H., and Howard, J. A. 1979. Developmental progression in play behavior of children between nine and thirty months: I. spontaneous play and imitation. *Developmental Medicine and Child Neurology* 21:299–310.

Leiter, R. G. 1969a. *Examiner's Manual for the Leiter International Performance Scale.* Chicago: Stoelting.

————. 1969b. *General Instructions for the Leiter International Performance Scale.* Chicago: Stoelting.

Leventhal, Bennett L. February 1983. Interview with author. Chicago, Illinois.

Levy, J., Meck, B., and Staikoff, J. 1978. "Dysfunction of the Left Cerebral Hemisphere in Autistic Children." Manuscript.

Levy, S. 1958. Projective figure drawing. In *The Clinical Application of Projective Drawings,* edited by E. F. Hammer, pp. 83–112. Springfield, Ill.: Thomas.

Lotter, V. 1966. Epidemiology of autistic conditions in young children: I. prevalence. *Social Psychiatry* 1:124–37.

Lovaas, O. I. 1977. *The Autistic Child.* New York: Wiley.

Lovaas, O. I., Schreibman, L., and Koegel, R. L. 1974. A behavior modification approach to the treatment of autistic children. *Journal of Autism and Childhood Schizophrenia* 4:111–29.

Lovitt, R., and Weiner, M. R. 1980. Conservation-withdrawal vs. depression in medically ill patients: Rorschach case study. *Journal of Personality Assessment* 44:460–64.

Luquet, H. G. 1913. *Les dessins d'un enfant: Etude psychologique* [*The Drawings of a Child: Psychological Study*]. Paris: Alcan.

————. 1920. Les bonhommes têtards dans le dessin enfantin [Tadpole figures in juvenile drawing]. *Journal de Psychologie Normale et Pathologique* 17:684–710.

————. 1927. *Le dessin enfantin* [*Juvenile Drawing*]. Paris: Alcan.

Machover, K. 1949. *Personality Projection in the Drawing of the Human Figure.* Springfield, Ill.: Thomas.

————. 1951. Drawing of the human figure: a method of personality investigation. In *An Introduction to Projective Techniques,* edited by H. H. Anderson and G. L. Anderson, pp. 341–69. New York: Prentice-Hall.

Massie, H. N. 1978. Blind ratings of mother-infant interaction in home movies of pre-psychotic and normal infants. *American Journal of Psychiatry* 135:1371–74.

Masters, R. E. L., and Houston, J. 1972. *Mind Games.* New York: Viking Press.

Melzack, R. 1973. *The Puzzle of Pain.* New York: Basic Books.

Meyer, A. P. 1957. *Psychobiology: A Science of Man.* Springfield, Ill.: Thomas.

Mize, R. 1980. Visual hallucinations following viral encephalitis: a self-report. *Neuropsychologia* 18:193–202.

Myklebust, H. R. 1954. *Auditory Disorders in Children*. New York: Grune & Stratton.

O'Gorman, G. 1970. *The Nature of Childhood Autism*. London: Butterworths.

Osofsky, J. D. 1979. *The Handbook of Infant Development*. New York: Wiley.

Piaget, J. [1947] 1950. *The Psychology of Intelligence*. Translated by M. Percy and D. E. Berlyne. London: Routledge & Kegan Paul. (Original work published in 1947 as *La psychologie de l'intelligence*. A. Colin, Paris.)

———. [1926] 1951*a*. *Judgment and Reasoning in the Child*. Translated by M. Warden. London: Routledge & Kegan Paul. (Original work published in 1926 as *Le jugement et le raisonnement chez l'enfant*. Delachaux & Niestlé, Neuchâtel.)

———. [1929] 1951*b*. *The Child's Conception of the World*. Translated by J. Tomlinson and A. Tomlinson. London: Routledge & Kegan Paul. (Original work published in 1929 as *La représentation du monde chez l'enfant*. F. Alcan, Paris.)

———. [1936] 1952. *The Origins of Intelligence in Children*. Translated by M. Cook. New York: International Universities Press. (Original work published in 1936 as *La naissance de l'intelligence chez l'enfant*. Delachaux & Niestlé, Neuchâtel.)

———. [1937] 1954. *The Construction of Reality in the Child*. Translated by M. Cook. New York: Basic Books. (Original work published in 1937 as *La construction du réel chez l'enfant*. Delachaux & Niestlé, Neuchâtel.)

———. [1926] 1955. *The Language and Thought of the Child*. Translated by M. Gabain. New York: World Publishing. (Original work published in 1926 as *Le langage et la pensée chez l'enfant*. Delachaux & Niestlé, Neuchâtel.)

———. [1952] 1957. *Logic and Psychology*. Translated by W. Mays. New York: Basic Books. (Original work based on three lectures at the University of Manchester in October 1952. Original work was in English.)

———. [1945] 1962. *Play, Dreams and Imitation in Childhood*. Translated by C. Gattegno and F. M. Hodgson. New York: Norton. (Original work published in 1945 as *La formation du symbole chez l'enfant*. Delachaux & Niestlé, Neuchâtel.)

———. [1946] 1969. *The Child's Conception of Time*. Translated by A. J. Pomerans. London: Routledge & Kegan Paul. (Original work published in 1946 as *Le développement de la notion de temps chez l'enfant*. Presses Universitaires de France, Paris.)

Piaget, J., and Inhelder, B. [1948] 1956. *The Child's Conception of Space.* Translated by F. J. Langdon and J. L. Lundzer. London: Routledge & Kegan Paul. (Original work published in 1948 as *La répresentation de l'espace chez l'enfant.* Presses Universitaires de France, Paris.)

———. [1966] 1969. *The Psychology of the Child.* Translated by H. Weaver. New York: Basic Books. (Original work published in 1966 as *La Psychologie de l'enfant.* Presses Universitaires de France, Paris.)

Richardson, A., and Cant, R. 1970. Eidetic imagery and brain damage. *Australian Journal of Psychology* 22:47–54.

Rimland, B. 1964. *Infantile Autism: The Syndrome and Its Implications for a Neural Theory of Behavior.* Englewood Cliffs, N.J.: Prentice-Hall.

———. 1968. On the objective diagnosis of infantile autism. *Acta Paedopsychiatrica* 35:146–61.

Riguet, C. B., Taylor, N. D., Benaroya, S., and Klein, L. S. 1981. Symbolic play in autistic, Down's and normal children of equivalent mental age. *Journal of Autism and Developmental Disorders* 11:439–48.

Ritvo, E. R., and Freeman, B. J. 1978. The National Society for Autistic Children's definition of the syndrome of autism. *Journal of the American Academy of Child Psychiary* 17:565–76.

Rojahn, J., McGonigle, J. J., Curcio, C., and Dixon, M. J. 1987. Suppression of pica by water mist and aromatic ammonia. *Behavior Modification* 1:65–74.

Rutter, M. 1968. Concepts of autism. *Journal of Child Psychology and Psychiatry* 9:1–25.

———. 1970. Autistic children: infancy to adulthood. *Seminars in Psychiatry* 2:435–50.

Rutter, M., Greenfield, D., and Lockyer, L. 1967. A five-to-fifteen-year follow-up study of infantile psychosis: II. social and behavioural outcome. *British Journal of Psychiatry* 13:1183–99.

Rutter, M., and Schopler, E., eds. 1978. *Autism, a Reappraisal of Concepts and Treatment.* New York: Plenum Press.

Scheerer, M., Rothmann, E., and Goldstein, K. 1945. A case of "idiot savant": an experimental study of personality organization. *Psychological Monographs* 58(4):1–63.

Schopler, E., and Mesibov, G. B., eds. 1983. *Autism in Adolescents and Adults.* New York: Plenum Press.

Seifert, C. D. 1988*a*. Learning from drawings: an autistic child looks out at us. *The American Journal of Art Therapy* 27(2):45–53.

———. 1988*b*. The human-figure drawing in the treatment of an autistic adolescent. *Child Psychiatry and Human Development* 19(1):74–81.

———. 1990*a*. *Theories of Autism.* Lanham, Md.: University Press of America.

———. 1990*b*. *Holistic Interpretation of Autism: A Theoretical Framework.* Lanham, Md.: University Press of America.

Selfe, L. 1977. *Nadia: A Case of Extraordinary Drawing Ability in an Autistic Child.* New York: Harcourt, Brace & Jovanovich.

Siipola, E. M., and Hayden, S. D. 1965. Exploring eidetic imagery among the retarded. *Perceptual and Motor Skills* 21:275–86.

Singh, M. M., Kay, S. R., and Pitman, R. K. 1981. Territorial behavior of schizophrenics. A phylogenetic approach. *Journal of Nervous and Mental Disease* 169:503–11.

Spitz, R. A. 1950. Anxiety in infancy. *International Journal of Psychoanalysis* 31:138–43.

————. 1959. *A Genetic Field Theory of Ego Formation.* New York: International Universities Press.

Stromeyer, C. F., III, and Psotka, J. 1970. The detailed texture of eidetic images. *Nature* 225:346–49.

Tanguay, P. E. 1984. Toward a new classification of serious psychopathology in children. *Journal of the American Academy of Child Psychiatry* 23:373–84.

Tennes, K., Emde, R., Kisley, A., and Metcalf, D. 1972. The stimulus barrier in early infancy: an exploration of some formulations of John Benjamin. In *Psychoanalysis and Contemporary Science,* vol. 1, edited by R. R. Holt and E. Peterfreund, pp. 206–34. New York: Macmillan.

Terman, L. M., and Merrill, M. A. 1973. *Stanford-Binet Intelligence Scale. Manual for the Third Revision Form L-M* (1972 norms ed.). 3rd ed., revised by M. A. Merrill. Boston: Houghton Mifflin.

Tinbergen, E. A., and Tinbergen, N. 1972. Early childhood autism: an ethological approach. *Beihefte zur Zeitschrift für Tierpsychologie* 10:1–53.

Traxel, W. 1962. Kritische Untersuchungen zur Eidetik [Critical examination of eidetic imagery]. *Archiv für die Gesamte Psychologie* 114:260–336.

Treffert, D. A. 1970. Epidemiology of infantile autism. *Archives of General Psychiatry* 22:431–38.

Trotter, R. J. 1983. Baby face. *Psychology Today* 17(8):14–20.

Wepman, J. M., Jones, L. V., Bock, R. D., and Van Pelt, D. 1960. Studies in aphasia: background and theoretical formulations. *Journal of Speech and Hearing Disorders* 25:323–32.

Whitehorn, J. C., and Zipf, G. K. 1943. Schizophrenic language. *Archives of Neurology and Psychiatry* 49:831–51.

Willemsen, E. 1979. *Understanding Infancy.* San Francisco: Freeman.

Wing, L. 1969. The handicaps of autistic children—a comparative study. *Journal of Child Psychology and Psychiatry* 10:1–40.

————. 1981. Asperger's syndrome: a clinical account. *Psychological Medicine* 11:115–29.

————. 1983. Social and interpersonal needs. In *Autism in Adolescents and*

Adults, edited by E. Schopler and G. B. Mesibov, pp. 337–53. New York: Plenum.

Wolf, D., and Gardner, H. 1979. Style and sequence in early symbolic play. In *Symbolic Functioning in Childhood,* edited by N. Smith and M. Franklin, pp. 117–38. Hillsdale, N.J.: Erlbaum.

Wolff, P. H. 1963. Developmental and motivational concepts in Piaget's sensorimotor theory of intelligence. *Journal of the American Academy of Child Psychiatry* 2:225–43.

Wolff, S., and Chick, J. 1980. Schizoid personality in childhood: a controlled follow-up study. *Psychological Medicine* 10:85–100.

Young, P. T. 1961. *Motivation and Emotion.* New York: Wiley.

Index

Abstract attitude
  defined, 32
  lack of, 20–21, 24, 30, 32–39, 42, 70, 71
  see also Imagination
Abstract thinking, 6
Adaptation. *See* Mother-child dyad; Self-actualization
Adolescents. *See* Kenneth; Ting
Affect, 5, 51–76, 99
  affective-cognitive symbiosis, 68–72, 100
  contact with normal children and, 75–76
  early attachments and, 51–61
  fear of strangers and, 53–54
  "flashlight," 55, 56
  interrelations and, 72, 75
  locating, 61–76
  mobilization and control, 62–67
  mother-child dyad and, 72–74
  surviving environmental stress and, 58–61
  see also Withdrawal
Affective development, 58, 61–62
  Brian, 59, 62, 63, 65, 68–72, 75–76
  Kenneth, 96
  Ting, 85, 90
Aholism, 68–69
American Psychiatric Association, 5, 92, 101
Anderson, R.B., 10, 74
Animal hypnosis, 59
Anthony, J., 79
Anxiety *vs.* fear, 53
Aphasia, 4, 42
  central, 19, 40
  mixed transcortical, 19, 42
  Ting, 84
Appley, M.H., 103n.
Arm flapping. *See* Hand/arm flapping
Assessment
  difficulty of, 67
  see also Diagnosis
Associative memory, 20, 42
Autism
  aphasia and, 4, 19, 40, 42, 84
  behavioral characteristics, 5–6
  brain abnormalities and, 2–3
  brain dysfunction and, cases of, 19, 33, 39–40, 42, 81
  case studies, 8; *see also* Brian; Kenneth; Ting
  defining, 5
  diagnosis, 3–4, 11–19, 100–101
  etiology, 2–3, 4, 99, 101

follow-up studies, 97–98
  heredity and, 3, 101
  holistic study of, 99
  identifying, 3–4, 11–19, 58, 100–101
  infancy, signs in, 1
  "infantile," 52, 58
  -normal continuum, 10, 52–53, 75
  organic. *See* Brain dysfunction
  organic causes, 2–3
  parents and, 2, 73–74, 77, 79
  prognosis for, 7–8, 97–98
  recognition, as disorder, 2
  retardation and, 4
  schizophrenia and, 4
  signs of, 1–2, 57
  statistics on, 5, 6, 7–8, 97
  stress and, 55, 58–61, 99
  treatment, 4, 7–8, 75–76, 98
Autism Society of America, 5
Aversion therapy, 7
Avoidance behavior, 59, 60, 71
  see also Withdrawal

Bauman, M., 3
Beery, K.E., 30
Behavioral characteristics, 5–6
Behavior modification, 7
Bell, C.C., 59
Bellak, L., 103n.
Bender, L., 30, 31, 68
Bender Visual Motor Gestalt Test. *See* Visual motor gestalt test
Benitone, J., 81
Benjamin, J.D., 55
Benson, D.F., 33
Bergman, P., 59
Berkson, G., 81
Bettelheim, B., 79, 100, 101
Birth
  Brian, 13
  Kenneth, premature, 91
  Ting, 83–84
Blomquist, H.K., 3
Body stiffening, 1
Brain abnormalities, 2–3
  Kenneth, 91
Brain dysfunction, 3, 5, 99
  cases of, 19, 33, 39–40, 42, 81
  see also Aphasia
Brain injury tests, 30, 31
Brask, B.H., 2

115

The Author

Cheryl D. Seifert trained in pediatric psychology at The University of Chicago, Wyler Children's Hospital, Department of Pediatrics, Pediatric Mental Development Clinic, Joseph P. Kennedy, Jr., Mental Retardation Center, and specialized in mental development and retardation. She held staff positions at The University of Chicago, Wyler Children's Hospital, Department of Pediatrics, Pediatric Psychological Services; Michael Reese Hospital and Medical Center, Dysfunctioning Child Center; and Mount Sinai Hospital Medical Center of Chicago, Department of Pediatrics, Pediatric Ecology Program.

She is the author of *Theories of Autism* and *Holistic Interpretation of Autism: A Theoretical Framework*.